FIOLET & WING:
An Anthology of Domestic Fabulist Poetry

Edited by
Stacey Balkun and Catherine Moore

Between the Lines
PUBLISHING

Between the Lines Publishing

Published by Between the Lines Publishing (USA)
as Liminal Books (imprint)
410 Caribou Trail, Lutsen, Minnesota 55612, USA

www.btwnthelines.com

Cover artist: Suzanne Johnson

Fiolet & Wing: An Anthology of Domestic Fabulist Poetry
Paperback ISBN: 978-1-950502-08-0

Table of Contents

Introduction

In "New Genres: Domestic Fabulism or Kansas with a Difference," published in *Electric Literature* in 2014, Amber Sparks defines "domestic fabulism" as writing that "takes the elements of fabulism—the animals that talk, the weather that wills itself into being, the people who can fly—and pulls them in tight, bringing them home." We see it in poetry as a disturbingly close-to-home magical realism; strange elements are dropped right into the most familiar-feeling poems.

Domestic fabulism is alluring to writers because it "creates a double existence, an anxiety that ends, if it does, in a sort of forced catharsis—we must confront the thing that lives in our house, in our marriage, in our family, in our town"—there's not exactly an exit from the story and not necessarily a "happily ever after." In editing this anthology, we gathered poetry from women using fabulist techniques as a means of writing deep anxieties: those so close to home they can barely be named. Domestic fabulism approaches these fears using magical elements "like a magnifying glass, or rather, a funhouse mirror" (Sparks).

As readers, we've found ourselves drawn to enchantment and fascinated by the way in which women's literature can drift into the mythological yet returns to the kitchen table, blending myth and magic with domestic concerns. Indeed, fabulism often amplifies the drama of the ordinary. This is not new; an appreciation for the melding of real and surreal elements has existed within our literary traditions for ages.

Within American poetry, we can trace this practice back to Emily Dickinson who wrote of discovering mermaids in the basement of the sea while on a walk along the shore. "I started Early – Took my Dog –" is one of Emily Dickinson's less commonly read poems. This may be due to its 'whimsical' tone. The poem appears simple enough at the literal level: a young girl walks to the shore with her dog, she enjoys herself until the tide catches her, then she becomes frightened and runs to the town for safety. It seems simple of course, except when the speaker contends with "Mermaids in the Basement," "Extended Hempen Hands," and an aggressive tide that "made as He would eat me up."

Dickinson's choice of broadened metaphors moves this poem between symbolic places— from the home, a place associated with safety and domesticity, to the sea, which is often a place of risk and adventure. The two conceits seem in contradiction to each other, a classic Dickinsonian style, to subvert and undermine each association that she creates.

The poem opens with an ordinary description of a walk at the seashore,

I started Early– Took my Dog—
And visited the Sea—

then quickly veers into something of strangeness and myth,

The Mermaids in the Basement
Came out to look at me —.

Throughout stanzas one and two, Dickinson uses house imagery to describe the sea and in this metaphor: the ocean bottom is the "Basement" and the surface is "the Upper Floor." The mermaids, sirens of sexual desire, are introduced here to hint at the oncoming intimate shift in narrative. Frigates filled with sailors' extended hands are resigned to the upper rooms clearly in physical separation; this is confirmed by stanza three's first line, "But no Man moved Me—till the Tide."

Beginning with stanza three, the sea is personified as a man and the poem expresses sexual implications. The speaker begins in innocence ("no Man Moved me"), presumably safe "till" she is sexually moved by "the Tide"—the man that completely engulfs her. The tide moves slowly up her body ("Went past my simple Shoe"), groping up her ankles. It moves higher still: "And past my Apron – and my Belt," and finally "past my Boddice – too." Is it getting hot in here? "And then – I started – too –/ And He – He followed – close behind." Indeed. The result of this movement is an "overflow" as beautiful as a "Pearl" released from its shell.

The use of the pronoun "we" in the poem's final stanza reiterates that the speaker and the sea are united, if for a moment. The last lines are lovely and a dignified dénouement in the sea's otherwise aggressive chase. Clearly separated, again, underlining the sexual content of the poem,

Until We met the Solid Town –
No One He seemed to know –
And bowing - with a Mighty look -
At me - The Sea withdrew –

Some critics suggest fear permeates the poem, a fear of love, where the sea is the symbol of a lover as it is in a number of Dickinson's early poems ("My river," "Wild night"), noting that the speaker may also fear her identity will be consumed by sexual experience as "a Dew" is taken up by the ocean. We would note that there is something rather calm in the final two lines; something has been sated or resigned. Perhaps this is joy, or regret of joy's loss, in the simple things that define the domestic— the dog, the house, the husband.

A few other things strike us about this poem. First, Dickinson did not live near the sea so the poem is not rooted in experience, as with the sensibilities of Elizabeth Bishop, a poet who would often take her dogs to shore then write of it. In fact, based on Dickinson's personal letters, this sea walk is completely imaginary, mermaids and all. Second, the narrative's plunge from the mundane to the magical, the intimate to the ethereal, within the poem was quite a radical writing approach for this time period, and a precursor of what would be to come in domestic fabulist genres. The fabulist elements in the poem may have confounded her contemporaries and later academic analyses, and in a highlight to the ways women's domestic writings have been dismissed, we end our discussion on Dickinson's poem with the following comment:

> ["I started Early—Took my Dog"] "The poem is abominable; and the quality of silly playfulness which renders it abominable is diffused more or less perceptibly throughout most of her work, and this diffusion is facilitated by the limited range of her metrical schemes." Yvor Winters, from his essay "Emily Dickinson and the Limits of Judgement"

In answer to such critics, we see the use of fabulist elements as a push-back against unspoken boundaries. These elements are neither silly nor whimsical, but a deliberate technique to express personal concerns without being directly biographical.

From the taboos of writing about 18th century intimacies to modern sexuality and gender role anxiety, we can trace the use of such components. Matthea Harvey's more recently published poems that dip into similar waters. Harvey's initial fascination with mermaids as subject matter is as she says, "because they're sex objects who can't have sex. Because there's a whole school of gender issues swimming around them." Her poems introduce us to a series of mermaids in domestic predicaments: drinking from a birdbath, being nipped at by a kitten, etc. As in Dickinson, when the magical elements drop away, we're left looking at a scene of domestic concern: a woman alone, trapped in an abrasive environment. Ultimately, we are compelled by the domestic issue at hand rather than by the mythical aspects of the piece.

Adding fabulism to a domestic story can elevate its characters to mythic levels, such as in Kelly Whiddon's "Riverbodies." In this poem, the speaker's Aunt Ella, who "lives at the river's edge," creates a sort of mythology in which the lead character commands over natural disasters and domestic spheres: "and when waters rise, she wades through her kitchen,/ skirts the snakes, and makes her breakfast of oatmeal/ and tabasco." Aunt Ella has a touch of witchiness. She handles the flood and still cooks a meal. She's not afraid of vermin, and when we think we'll get some honey, she gives us hot sauce instead. She is fabulous: a creature straight out of a folk or fairy legend.

iii

Folk tales have been doing the work of writing the difficult for ages. These complex conversations, such as warning our daughters upon the onset of their maturation in "Little Red Riding Hood," take place in quintessential cautionary tales. Under the cloak of an old German fable, we have a coming-of-age story in which the protagonist is a mere babe in the woods of a cross-dressing wolf. She's an innocent who forgot to walk the straight path to grandmother's house and, therefore, learns a dreadful lesson on being chaste and chased. As Catherine Orenstein reminds us in her pivtol book *Little Red Riding Hood Uncloaked*, the sexual undertones are remarkable for a children's story and the moral imperative for young girls is clear: do as you are told or fall to the predator. While this may not be the adolescent advice we'd like to bestow in modern times, we understand it within its historical legacy, and are often saddened by contemporary attitudes that still seem to foster "rape culture" thinking which holds the victim responsible for their own attack. Even now, Little Red should be wary in the hood.

Fabulism no doubt has its roots in folk tales such as Little Red. To quote Amber Sparks once more, such tales offer a total "immersion, an exploration of self and situation—of the dread that lives and lurks at home, where we cannot escape it." Maybe the dread has always existed entangled in domestic life, perhaps paralyzing the poet's inability to express it, but domestic fabulism gives the poet a new approach to letting unspeakable topics slip into the narrative. Maybe this apprehension has something to do with a feeling of foreboding in giving words free rein and of a sense that, historically, women have never been allowed the same freedoms of men.

In that vein, we open the *Fiolet & Wing* anthology with Sarah Brown Weitzman's "Forbidden," a poem ripe with historic texts and tales:

> There's always been something forbidden
> to women
> apples
> a last look
> at Sodom and Gomorrah

Weitzman shows us the breadth of what's been forbidden to women before sharpening her focus on a single text. She then imagines the life of Bluebeard's bride:

> When she could sleep
> she dreamed of bolts
> thrown back
> latches lifted.

The poem continues, describing "the graphic insertion" of a key into a lock of which she dreamed most often. The re-appropriation of this familiar tale and its method of examining the main character's inner-life, isn't quite magical realism. It isn't quite realistic, either. Still, it not only reads as domestic fabulism but as an allegory for what this genre can do for writers, especially those of marginalized groups:

> Yet it wasn't what she'd expected
> when it finally happened
> to her nor
> is it for any of us
> when we open the door of an unlit room
> and see the dark leap back
> to make space for us.

Turning to this magical, mythological, mysterious realm of the ultra-familiar is an opening of a doorway where, rather than finding an enclosed closet space, a new world appears. This broadening makes room for transformative moments, and there, on that segment of literary carpet, that threshold between worlds, is where the poetry of this genre lies.

The contemporary poems collected here do not shy from the forbidden and do not look away. They take the mundane to mythic heights by not only drawing from historic texts but by using techniques such as shifting in Animorphism, creating tension with fabled character, narrative, and place, and weaving magic into the most unlikely scenarios. *Fiolet & Wing* traces the use of fabulism from Weitzman's poem, first published in 1982, to ultra-contemporary poetry. These poems have come from women writing all over the world and exhibit a wide range of experience, voice and style. However, each poem explores the mythology of the mundane, investigating themes of domestic work, family, and relationships. These poems take place in kitchens, backyards, neighborhood pools, and fitting rooms. Narratives unfold while speakers change for gym class, shop for groceries, cook, and eat holiday meals. These are poems of womanhood and otherness, of puberty, childbirth, menopause, and everything in between.

Emotional and bodily changes are often marked by animalistic metaphor. As its title implies, M. Brett Gaffney's "Butterfly Girl" likens adolescent girls to insects. They "all remember the transformation" into their new bodies, that beauty and discomfort. Gaffney spins the anxiety of a high school locker room into myth:

> They quickly dress for gym and fly from the room,
> knowing it's best to let alone an empty cocoon,
> dripping wings.

With many contemporary offerings, like Gaffney and others, Animorphism may seem like a trend, although it is an old tradition in terms of folklore and myth (along with the narrative dread of what may live and lurk at home).

Similarly, many domestic fabulist poems place unlikely characters in familiar spaces. In "The Fates Hang Wallpaper" by Elizabeth Vignali, these white-robed determiners of destiny are busied with hanging wallpaper, an especially mundane task compared to their power and skills. Referring to both wallpaper and the fate of the universe, they say:

> We slacken, we straighten.
> We cut. If we do our job right (and we always do),
> you'll never know it could have been otherwise.

Susan J. Erickson's "Venus de Milo Gets Ready for the Halloween Party" humorously places us directly into an anxiety-ridden scene of a woman getting ready for a party, where we commiserate with the idea that no costume can ever really conceal us, through Venus's thoughts:

> The missing arms were a dead give away.
> I'd need sleeves to cover youthful sins.

In poems like these, domestic fabulism works to create a spectacular tension (and a lot of fun) within the small confines of a poem.

Fabulist elements allow a different kind of pretend by letting a writer look her subject in the eye, but from a comfortable distance. Akua Lezli Hope's "Cook" turns a kitchen into a "space/ between eternities" in which a woman explores her infertility through what could be made from an egg: "what this / shattering may yield, / will flan, waffle, pancake." Likewise, Shelley Puhak's "Letter to the Gnome Who Stole My Firstborn" stealthily deals with bargaining in the raw emotional state after an unexpected loss of a baby. Tammy Bendetti's "2.3" takes a darker look at infertility by examining the spills and humid ickiness representational of the dirt growing in an "average" household. A household is traditionally completed by the average 2.3 children, but here, while mildew grows in the kitchen towels and mosquitoes spawn in the backyard, the speaker's womb "will fruit only teeth."

Many domestic fabulist poems operate with a clear sense of familiarity of place. Place is so important. It operates like a character in many of these poems—it creates the juxtaposition, tension, and strength that can take a reader by surprise. "Menopause at the Market" reclaims the supermarket of Allen Ginsberg and uses its sexual imagery to explore the sexuality of an aging woman. Because we have all seen the "bin of tomatoes" and "ripe avocados" gleaming in a grocery store, we are familiar with the setting and pleasantly surprised when the poem pushes into an imagined narrative. Sarah Ann Winn explores loss of place in "Last House Screen Door" which features the scene of a house completely fallen into the sea. Oddly, individual parts remain intact, just like with our most cherished memories. Even in loss, some items never waver: "Somehow the cake stand survived the tumble."

A fabulist collection would be incomplete without the inclusion of fairytale poetry and we are happy to include poems that use fabled devices in a variety of degrees. Specifically, when fairytale elements are dropped into familiar domestic spaces, readers approach the poem with the preset themes and archetypes of its chosen allusion. This literary relationship allows the poet to complement or contradict the original material's intent. Wendy Carlisle's "Snow White Explains" offers an unhappy version on being a lone female surrounded by all men: "Try to imagine my danger—." In "We Are All Her Grandmother" by Eileen Malone, the collective 'we' have already been consumed by the wolves of this world and sadly possess the age-given wisdom that "eventually red riding hood/ will succumb, it's just a matter/ of story." In yet another switch of generational perspective, Mercedes Webb-Pullman creates a younger speaker who regrets the forgotten magic of her grandmother in her poem "Grendel." Each of these pieces pulls elements from and moves further in conversation with their sourced tales.

As one can see, a contemporary poem does not need to fully re-visit existing material; often, just a lifting of the merest thread from our folk-cannon adds a unique layering to many of the poems in this collection. Hijacking literary characters and placing them in everyday modern experiences is another approach to conjoin the fabulist and the domestic. We delight in the wickedness of hand-cleaning questions in "Lady Macbeth On Call-in Radio" by Dori Appel. We want to offer our own two cents as Erin Elizabeth Smith's "Alice Gives Advice to Dorothy" imagines two magical characters together discussing domestic battles between the sexes.

Then there are the poems with uncategorized magical otherness. Somehow, the completely ordinary world is utterly infused with magic, which both grounds us while surprising us. E. Kristin Anderson's "Tupperware Party" imagines "If my body is a Tupperware party,/ I'll let my tongue speak for itself," dropping us into a domestic scene and yet taking agency over the situation. As Susan Rich's poem "Tricks a Girl Can Do" reminds us, women can make magic out of anything. And in these poems, the girls certainly make things, from modern love potions in "Star Anise" (Carol Guess) and "Witching" (Robin Sams) to households filled with objects under spells in "Domiciliary Diaspora" (Jenny MacBain-Stephens). In these otherworlds, our landscapes might talk ("If the ocean had a Mouth" by Marie-Elizabeth Mali) or a dress might take flight to whisk off the poem's speaker ("A Woman Might Way to Fly, Away" by Jennifer Givhan). In each imagined world, some traditionally domestic metaphor twists magically, turning the concrete fabulist.

As many of these fabulist poems do, Emari DiGiorgio's "The Treed Lady" begins with an all too familiar and hurtful scenario: "When the boy in my bible class planted a wad / of Bazooka Joe at the root of my skull." In this moment, we feel powerless along with the speaker, until the magic arrives: "he didn't / expect a sapodilla to grow." The growth of this tree gives our speaker agency and despite the hardships caused by this differentiating element, we learn "there are ways to live / with the gifts we've been given." PaulA Neves offers an equally lush and magical world in "Capricornucopia," in which goats visit our speaker's family for a holiday dinner. "Like midnight buffet tourists,"--that is, the unwanted? Or insatiable? Both. These goats "charged the sweetmeats, the Mouton Cadet, / the *chanfana* like grandma used to make," ultimately becoming cannibals by feasting on this traditional Portuguese goat dish. Our poor speaker who has done her best to accommodate these intrusive visitors, with the eloquently and cadence of a hymnal merely allows the magic to conflate back into the domestic scene: "Let them. / Let them be goats. / Let them eat everything— / even the bones."

We are proud to showcase poems collected by so many women all over the world; each poet arrives at fabulism in her own way. Outside of the U.S. we received submissions from Canada, UK, Ireland, France, Germany, Australia, New Zealand, India, Albania, and Bangladesh. Even though we did not require geography identification, we feel this project naturally attracted work from a lot of English-speaking women across the globe writing about the domestic in various fabulist styles. As a result, *Fiolet & Wing* readers will experience the world through the domestic fabulist poetry of international writers. They will become mesmerized by the Iranian folklore interwoven as "Home Remedy" in Ellen Estilai's sestina. Foreign landscapes permeate through poem narratives: Australia in "Change of Plans" (Jane Frank), India in "History's Private Life" (Nandini Dhar), and others. If the collection had been open to translated work, we are certain it could have doubled in size.

Despite the wide range of content, form, and voice, there is a collectiveness resonant in these poems. In a way, the poetry we've collected is that of reaching for a sense of belonging. How else but through the domestic fabulist could women tell their innermost stories, the ones that barely make sense in our own heads? How else could writers accurately portray the emotional overload of the domestic sphere?

This is not to say there is a specific way to handle these subjects in this genre. As editors, we had an eye for selecting a menagerie of technique and style for poets working in domestic fabulism. We read many excellent poems that covered the spectrum from realistic domesticity to the most surreal fabulism. To find the sweet spot balanced in the middle was a challenge. The selection process was difficult, and *Fiolet & Wing* certainly does not set out to define domestic fabulist work but to enter and further open the conversation of myth and magic in contemporary women's literature. It showcases a range of voices that will emphasize the flexibility, diversity, and strength of domestic fabulist poetry.

According to R. T. Smith in "Thriving on Buck & Wing," the afterword of a special issue of *Shenandoah*, "Poets who have a song and a story, a history and a language etched into the land are likely to have a vision which includes the idea of a poem as a ceremony" (207). The poems we have collected revel in song and story; they are poems of ritual and celebration, observance and procedure, even performance, to an extent. These poems resonate off the page where the fabulist elements can disturb the familiarity of history and vision to turn the mundane into myth, ceremonies grounded in everyday actions.

Stacey Balkun and Catherine Moore
    The Editors, *Fiolet & Wing: An Anthology of Domestic Fabulist Poetry*

Further Citations [in order of appearance]

"I started Early—took my Dog" reprinted electronically by permission of the publishers and the Trustees of Amherst College from The Poems of Emily Dickinson, Thomas H. Johnson, ed. J520, Cambridge, Mass.: The Belknap Press of Harvard University Press, Copyright © 1951, 1955, 1979, 1983 by the President and Fellows of Harvard College. Source: *The Poems of Emily Dickinson Edited by R.W. Franklin* (Harvard University Press, 1999).

Yvor Winters from "Emily Dickinson and the Limits of Judgement," In Defense of Reason, 3rd ed. (Denver: Alan Swallow, 1947), p. 284.

"Mermaid Convention: An Interview with Matthea Harvey" By Stephen Burt, *The Paris Review.* September 2, 2014.

Catherine Orenstein, *Little Red Riding Hood Uncloaked: Sex, Morality and the Evolution of a Fairy Tale.*

Forbidden

Sarah Brown Weitzman

There's always been something forbidden
to women
apples
a last look
at Sodom and Gomorrah
that box left at Pandora's.

Bluebeard's latest bride wore a ring
of keys at her side.
Honeymoon and the weeks after
opening locks
entering rooms
inspecting the contents
but in the central corridor
of her attention
the one door her husband denied her.

Nor could the key be ignored
bumping bruises into her hip
snagging her silks
thrusting itself into her hand
whenever she reached for one of the others.

Nights it kept her awake.
When she could sleep
she dreamed of bolts
thrown back
latches lifted.
But it was fitting
a key into a lock
she dreamed of most
the graphic insertion
the twists
that climaxed in her waking.

Yet it wasn't what she'd expected
when it finally happened
to her nor
is it for any of us
when we open the door of an unlit room
and see the dark leap back
to make space for us.

Sarah Brown Weitzman has had work in hundreds of journals and anthologies including *The New Ohio Review*, *Poet & Critic*, *The North American Review*, *Rattle*, *Mid-American Review*, *Ekphrasis*, *Poet Lore*, *Spillway*, and others. Sarah received a Fellowship from the National Endowment for the Arts. A departure from poetry, her fourth book, *Herman and the Ice Witch*, is a children's novel published by Main Street Rag. Her latest chapbook, *Looking Back*, is forthcoming from Finishing Line Press.

A Woman Might Want to Fly, Away

Jennifer Givhan

After my salt bath after watching
the evening sky the way one watches

birds, I reached for my favorite dress, its
slimming V, when I saw that its crossed back

had grown a pair of wings. I carried it
flapping to the medicine cabinet, pulled out

tiny eyebrow scissors & began clipping
like loose threads from a hem, only thicker

& wilder. Then I slipped the dress
over my head, examined my reflection:

the diet was working, but slowly
as a winter fog, lifting. I turned—

the wings. Only now they were beating
madly & soon I began to fly.

My husband was working late.
I called to my children, but the door

was closed or they pretended
not to hear & I couldn't control

the dress—I tried lifting it over my head
but it was stronger & carried me

toward the balcony glass
slamming me, again & again

until I unfumbled the latch.
The night fell cool.

She felt herself much lighter
I said aloud so the dress could hear, sure

it was listening. Was another woman watching
as I blended into sunset, dipping from sight?

At last I grew tired of flying & hunger & cold.
I struggled. The dress fell into a patch

of superstition mallow at a field's edge—
I, nearly naked, beside it.

A teenager on a bike lent me his phone
so I called my mother who said

she understood. It wasn't just dresses
but any clothing. *Once a woman's reached*

a certain age? I asked. No, it was
the watching, she said, handing me a wrap.

Jennifer Givhan, a Mexican-American poet and novelist, has earned NEA and PEN/Rosenthal Emerging Voices fellowships. Her books include *Rosa's Einstein* (2019 Camino Del Sol Poetry Series), and two novels, *Trinity Sight* and *Jubilee* (Blackstone Publishing). Her honors include the Frost Place Latinx Scholarship and fifteen Pushcart nominations. Her work has appeared in *Best New Poets*, *Poetry Daily*, *Verse Daily*, *POETRY*, and *The Kenyon Review*. She lives near the Sleeping Sister volcanoes in New Mexico with her family, and can be found discussing feminist motherhood at jennifergivhan.com, Facebook, & Twitter @JennGivhan.

The Woman Whistles

Sarah Gerkensmeyer

The woman stands beside her house and whistles for something, her hands caught up in her apron. She whistles, and her hands are caught up in the damp fabric of her apron, holding the entire weight of her worry and working at it there. First a child comes trotting up the lane, a tightly swaddled baby in a basket that smells like cloves. The woman barely glances at the warm, mewling bundle before looking back out toward the furthest horizon and whistling for something again. A unicorn comes trotting up the lane. The woman keeps whistling. Her husband comes trotting up the lane. Her ex-husband comes trotting up the lane. Her two dead husbands come trotting up the lane. She whistles. A sycamore tree, its bark mottled and smeared and beautiful, comes trotting up the lane. The woman glances at the tree and then whistles yet again. Three swans come trotting up the lane. Her dog comes trotting up the lane. A typewriter comes trotting up the lane. The woman whistles. Her mother comes trotting up the lane, three fat suitcases in tow. Her sister and five sickly elves come trotting up the lane. The woman closes her eyes and concentrates. She whistles. An ocean—tiny fish and large fish darting and shimmering in the clear, rising crests of waves—comes trotting up the lane. All of Paris comes trotting up the lane: warm, crusty baguettes hopping, the Eiffel Tower jigging. The woman whistles. Her best friend from childhood comes trotting up the lane, clutching against her that impossible, solid feeling that they used to have when they were alone together: that they were the only ones. The woman opens her eyes and watches the horizon and whistles. Her dreams come trotting up the lane, and they quiver when she looks at them for just one second before fixing her gaze on the horizon once more. She whistles. All of it comes trotting up the lane. Every last thing comes trotting up the lane. The whole ball of wax, the whole enchilada, the whole lot, and the whole shebang come trotting up the lane. The echo of her own whistle, even, comes trotting up the lane and returns to her as one long, plaintive sound that she must catch in her apron and hold tight against her belly until it is still and rigid and then finally soft and thin and as empty as air.

Sarah Gerkensmeyer's story collection *What You Are Now Enjoying* was selected by Stewart O'Nan as winner of the 2012 Autumn House Press Fiction Prize, longlisted for the Frank O'Connor International Short Story Award, and chosen as winner of Late Night Library's Debut-litzer Prize. A Pushcart Prize nominee for both fiction and poetry and a finalist for the Katherine Anne Porter Prize in Short Fiction and the Italo Calvino Prize for Fabulist Fiction, Sarah has received scholarships to the Bread Loaf Writers' Conference, Ragdale, Grub Street, SAFTA's Firefly Farms, and the Vermont Studio Center. Her stories and poetry have appeared in *American Short Fiction, Guernica, The New Guard, The Massachusetts Review, Hayden's Ferry Review, B O D Y, Hobart,* and *Cream City Review,* among others. Her story "Ramona" was featured in a *Huffington Post* piece on flash fiction and also selected by Lily Hoang for the 2014 Best of the Net Anthology. Sarah was the 2012-13 Pen Parentis Fellow. She received her MFA in fiction from Cornell University and now lives and writes in her home state of Indiana, where she is a finalist for the 2016 Indiana Authors Award in the emerging category. Currently, she is a Sustainable Arts Fellow.

Ode to a Parallel Universe in Which I Make My Point

Catherine Kyle

In the house where we live above the opera singer,
I pour out whiskey while you burn photographs.

Photographs of ships. Of your first wedding day.
Purple smoke rising from bowl. The liquor hits

the drain. I dreamed I was an exorcist slaying all
your poltergeists. I dreamed we came to earth to

make something good together. But dreams,
as we know, are just minnows. We haven't left

the house for days. Downstairs she sings
Ave Maria. The fireflies are hatching all over

the streets. And kids crackle fireworks in alleys.
We communicate in toasts to what has been

broken. The day we climbed the tree. The day
we danced in a descending elevator. Dreams:

just poltergeists. Tonight you grab me by the
hair and seethe into my cochlea: *I don't know if*

I want to slap you or screw you. Maybe I want to do
both. But I am a minnow. I slip through your grip.

I wriggle out of your fingers. I fishtail down
the hall. Water rises from the drain to baptize all

your scorch marks. Wind rises from the west and

scrapes the roof off clean. Upstairs your flint eyes

are catching God's fire. Downstairs she bellows words
above the swirling gale. *Ave Maria. Benedictus.* Blessed.

Catherine Kyle is the author of the forthcoming *Shelter in Place* (Spuyten
Duyvil), *Saint: A Post-Dystopian Hagiography* (dancing girl press, 2018),
Parallel (Another New Calligraphy), *Flotsam* (Etched Press), *Gamer: A Role-
Playing Poem* (dancing girl press), and *Feral Domesticity* (Robocup Press). Her
writing has been honored by the Idaho Commission on the Arts, the Alexa Rose
Foundation, and other organizations. She holds a Ph.D. in English from
Western Michigan University and is pursuing an MFA in Poetry through New
England College's low-residency program. She teaches creative writing at the
College of Western Idaho and through The Cabin, a literary nonprofit. Her
website is www.catherinebaileykyle.com.

Variations on a Domestic Theme

Anna Lowe Weber

i.

Nine a.m., and the wife has been awake
for hours already.

She has clipped chrysanthemums
from the side yard garden
and placed the buds in a bud vase.

She has washed a load of wash.

She watches the neighborhood children,
steals their sidewalk chalk
when they move indoors at noon for lunch.

Her own refrigerator bears half a melon
like a split planet that can't help but expose
its slick, seeded core. Pervert.

ii.

Afternoons give way to a strange quiet
in the house.

When the wife wakes from her nap, the trees
have traded their leaves for mosquito netting,
white fibers and knots.

Things to chop: carrots
           onions
           garlic
           cabbage
           leeks

turnips
shank,
(a word
she hates
for no real reason at all.)

What she'll have in one to two hours: scotch broth.

iii.

Sometime between light and dark,
the husband returns, newspaper
tucked under his arm.

He searches for his keys, clumsy pat down.
Under the porch light, he is a tragic figure,
a ham-fisted provider.
Still, his overcoat glows a little.

They have scotch broth.
They have evening now, utterly.
The call of the neighborhood children
as they prowl yards without permission,
and faces at the window like moons in masks.

iv.

Lieutenant Darkness sets up camp
throughout the house.

Around midnight, like the careless release
of a balloon from a child's loose fist,
the house rises.

The wife knows this happens occasionally,
but cannot say how or why.

In the air, nothing changes but the altitude.
The husband's breath still has an evenness
that burns the insides of her eyes.
A robe is still a robe.
A cup of tea, still tea.

v.

Like a cat at the lips of a newborn,
something sucks the air from the house
and it begins its descent.

Afternoons at the park,
the wife has watched
patient mothers open their arms
at the bottom of the big yellow slide and wait

with smiles wide as an open tent flap.
In this way too, daybreak waits for the house.

Still, like a child, the house hovers,
not quite ready to come down just yet.
The house, a wayfarer. Darkling.
A pilgrim soul.

Anna Lowe Weber's poetry has appeared in *Ninth Letter, Iowa Review, Tar River Poetry*, the *Florida Review*, and *Salamander*, among other journals, and she has a chapbook, *Blessing for the Unborn*, from Finishing Line Press. She currently resides in Alabama with her husband and two children where she teaches creative writing at the University of Alabama in Huntsville.

2.3

Tammy Bendetti

The weather's dry here, darling.
I had to improvise.
The air roils,
boiling pots on the range.
The tap runs unvalved
onto your
travertine tiles.
Towels mildew.
Spider ferns overspill their pots,
the orchids riot.
Electronics glitch and drip.
Mosquitos spawn
in the basement pond,
and the morning you wake
eye to eye with a tree frog
perched on the bedpost,
you will regret the blood
in the garden. My womb
will fruit only teeth.

Tammy Bendetti is a tiny, loud, queer poet living in Colorado with her husband and daughters. When she's not writing, she's probably selling houses, painting, or having weird dance parties with her kids. You can find her recent work in *Fire Poetry*, *Alyss*, and *Whale Road Review*. Lithic Press published her first chapbook, *Poison in Small Doses*, in 2018.

Madame Butterfly

Kristin Chang

That summer you compared my breasts
to dumplings I learned how to butcher

a horse. How to birth a blade
and call it marriage, how to be

something in the mouth, like a peach.
Your OkCupid profile says you

want an Asian girl, a wife-like lip
and long hair in a braid, you say you know

how I want it, you've memorized a scene
you saw in a movie once, a pair of knees

like moons and a dragonfly mask, the point is to
be beautiful the way something easily

crushed is beautiful. You want me clean
as a bone, you want a skin to shine

a skin to rhyme with a ghost you
spat from your boot heel, you want a

kind of pain only a man who has never
known pain can pray for. My braid is a flute and my

blood in a soup bowl is my wife, is the sky, is when the
sky saw us through a window and lost face,

your favorite condom brand is Japanese, Kimono
XXX, my skin worn on your fist.

Fiolet & Wing

What body cannot be collapsed like a paper
parasol, what body cannot be loaded like a paper

pistol, my face powdered and yours cocked,
I sink into this body I called my own

by mistake. Redness surfacing on my upper lip
like a body mid-river. The sky asks permission to occupy

me and it doesn't care what comes next.
The clouds snagging on these hands

you said made your own look so big. That
summer I dreamed of a Chinese woman who

drowned in my backyard river, who saddled my
mouth with hers and bridled every bankside body

sunning clam-pink. The reins in her mouth
like a tongue. We tucked the water under our chins

and I told her I could learn to occupy any kind of meat,
to prove it I flashed her my horse thigh and her

muzzle bobbed like a fleet, she stitched a steak
to my left ear and called it mothering instinct.

That summer I fell asleep twice in the birdbath,
a dragonfruit strangled between my thighs, pulp

storming my tongue like a visiting army. I
emptied each warhorse into my mouth, licked

the bullet that recalls the belly, wore
the belly as a costume. How the body

unlearns itself: unspooling into smoke
against my palms, I watch

the bullets that stack all along your breath,
blasting new holes
nothing like moons
into this skin, this violence we've learned to call song.

Kristin Chang's work has been published in *Teen Vogue, Muzzle Magazine, The Margins* (Asian American Writers Workshop), the *Shade Journal*, and elsewhere. Her work has been nominated multiple times for Best of the Net and Best New Poets. She works for *Winter Tangerine* and can be found online at kristinchang.com and on Twitter (@KXinming). She is passionate about martial arts films and matriarchy.

The Conceit of Nesting Dolls

Megan McSparren Parker

Tell me how you would take me apart—
Would you unscrew me piece by piece, tease
my breasts from torso, pluck pubes
with precise nails, strip my thigh

flesh with your teeth?
Then I would be hollow for you,
as hollow as those Russian dolls you stack
around the house. You know the ones—

A girl inside a girl inside a girl. Sometimes
inside a boy. My favorite
is the peasant with her blue apron strings.
She is mother, "little matron."

She is what I wear to unload dishes, to pound
chicken breasts into piccata, to pour you
scotch or screwdriver.
She was who I felt with each deep

violet contraction in both delivery rooms.
The white lines by her hooded eyes
belong to me,
and I cake them with concealer.

Within her is the scarlet woman (your favorite)—
I know because you always thumb her
painted cleavage when the kids
free her from your nightstand, and you

put her back in her place. Sometimes
I feel her in a hitch of breath,
in a pink prickled heat along

my clavicle. Rarely

do you unstack her. I understand. She's hard
to reach inside the womb of one
who is mistress of mucus and tantrums,
who hasn't time for screwing.

But that's ok.
These breasts are suckled sore anyway.

Megan McSparren Parker works as a freelance editor and as an adjunct for
UC Berkeley Extension. Her fiction and poetry have been published in *Harpur
Palate*, *The Writing Disorder*, *The Sonder Review*, and *FLARE*, among others,
and her flash fiction piece, "A Good Thing," was the tertiary winner of SNHU's
Fall 2016 Short Fiction Contest. Currently, she resides outside of San Antonio,
TX with her husband and two daughters, where she's revising her first YA novel
and drafting new poetry. She can be found lurking on Twitter from time to time
@MegsMcSparren.

Tupperware Party

E. Kristin Anderson

If my body is a Tupperware party,
I'll let my tongue speak for itself. Look—
how perfectly sealed I can be. Look—
how easily opened. Pass around my fingers
like melon ballers. Examine my toes
like a good set of measuring spoons
on a perfect ring. Dishwasher safe, lifetime
guaranteed. I see your pretty dresses:
starched, fluffed, matching your lipstick.
My lipstick is the whisper of an air-tight seal.
My dress is a pasta strainer, and I will fade—
not break, not warp or bend—over the next
twenty years. If my body is a Tupperware party,
I am not invited. And yet, here I am,
in a stranger's living room, my shoulders
distributed as door prizes, raffled off
and grasped in nervous-sweaty hands. I close
my eyes and wait for these women to finish
their finger sandwiches and petit fours. Wait
to pick up the paper plates, watch them collapse
into an old trash compactor, its rumble
visceral and sweet.

Based in Austin, TX, **E. Kristin Anderson** has been published widely in magazines. She's also the author of eight chapbooks, including *A Guide for the Practical Abductee, Fire in the Sky* and *Pray, Pray, Pray: Poems I wrote to Prince in the middle of the night.* Kristin is Special Projects Manager for ELJ and a poetry editor at *Found Poetry Review*. Once upon a time she worked at *The New Yorker*.

Domiciliary Diaspora

Jennifer MacBain-Stephens

The house, a predator box,
inhales, tenses to pounce:
all the little babies
scatter across the tile.

1. Shower Curtain
   Tear the material first. Skin is meant to slough.
   Rouge and olive tones signify something borrowed,
   something born, red platelets cluster, the lawn monster,
   unflinching. I confront the shower curtain.
Pretend you weren't born to suffocate.

2. Quilt
   Slithers out of the hall closet. A counter intuitive turban the way
   of *swoosh* all super hero language holes up in the dust ruffle.
   It wants to secure around necks,
no needles for the face holes, the neediest eaten alive, stabs at air.
forgets victims post storm, accordion of wonder bread smell.

3. Accessory
Sterling necklace chokes a soft flesh
hallow, this hallow no good anymore,
the grip determined, it's not even close to finished.

4. Garbage Disposal
Easy listening screams.
Sturm und Drang ravages delicacies.
Ska drowns out the dying and the growing.
The underground, happened.

5. Cloth
A little white dress pirouettes
in the center of the bedroom.

A green flannel shirt, pulls an all nighter,
smokes a cigarette, grabs the dress's
armless arms, dances his point home.

6.   Air Conditioning Unit
Propped up like a school photo,
stood up all by himself at the plate,
guarded the bases, tried to be a good temperate
manager but lost it all at the track,
lumbers up and down sound cavities,
imprisons starts and stops.

7.   Table
Recovering.
My legs feel asleep
They are unhinged.
They are lying next to you.
Hardware in a Zip lock bag,
mourns it's solid personality away.

8.   Chairs
Scream in panic from inside a van.
If you lose your guidebook, do not panic.
"Someone turn on the lights."
You are going to a better place.
Only the objects hear me,
no one speaks to me.

9.   Lazy Boy
Most wanted posters go up around town.
Too lazy to mouth help, to be found.
The breadcrumbs,
the broken foot rest,
rusty hinges, a confusing stain,
dimes, popcorn kernels nestle in
for dusk's double cry feature.

10. Lost cat,
found, like any
dark creature that worships the
          keyboard corners of ourselves.

11. Picture Frame,
Out past curfew,
discovered in a Hefty bag,
the wood scratched:
glue cannot mend.
Hold the pieces together.
No, it cannot be mended.
Hold them together.
Again.
No. It cannot.

12. Bullhorn
is introduced,
sirens wail,
     Arrests are made.

13. Photo Album
     vivisected, plastic sheens
sliced bit by bit, thrown down a
     laundry chute by someone
unsupervised.

14. Camping Equipment
    ravaged   by a   hippie.

15.
It happens faster.

    16.Monogrammed Stationary
thrown into the fire, a ritual killing.

           17. The crockery
remains stoic.

   -4. Loss.

-10. More loss. But we gain spirituality.

22

3. A Block
> of wood
> on the porch.
>> magic marker scratched
> out its face, its confident life rings.

4. A Fish
> stick in the microwave,
the door only opens from the outside,

anticipates annihilation.

We are so technologically advanced
says the barista,
with full bean flavor.
I sit at the counter,
the last object.

Jennifer MacBain-Stephens lives in the Midwest and is the author of four full length poetry collections: *Your Best Asset is a White Lace Dress* (Yellow Chair Press), *The Messenger is Already Dead* (Stalking Horse Press), *We're Going to Need a Higher Fence,* tied for first place in the 2017 Lit Fest Book Competition, and *The Vitamix and the Murder of Crows* is recently out from Apocalypse Party. Her work has been nominated for Best of the Net and the Pushcart Prize. She is also the author of ten chapbooks. Recent work can be seen at or is forthcoming from *The Pinch, Black Lawrence Press, Quiddity, Prelude, Cleaver, Yalobusha Review,* and *Inter/rupture.* Visit: http://jennifermacbainstephens.wordpress.com.

Ode to the Bobbin and the Spool

Robin Carstensen

The refrigerator quietly flaps
against the floor, taps the walls of this old brick
      apartment, clicks and chortles like the gas
heater from time to time, rumbling back
to life as if remembering a tale.
      When the green dogwood reigned, I was your knight
upon a winged mare; we built a castle,
drew a bridge across the moat.
      How you beckoned me across. How your red cloak
gathered after the mystery of us.
Oh, how you played the queen brilliantly, once
      writing how affairs of state
could not distract you from the horizon,
gazing for me from your windowpane.

      Morning sweeps the geese into Oklahoma
morning two hours before
it fans the foothills in El Cajon.
      Our letters take longer to reach, fewer
and fewer as our castle fades in the fog,
the bridge strains to come down, the moat
      extends its berth, your bristling red gown
trails after life and the regular state
of affairs, my mare plods old ground.
      Another weekend morning, quiet phone.
When I call, you are sewing a dress,
and I am learning not to be jealous
      of your loose attentions—thread unraveling
your breath behind the piston thud-shuffle-thumping
      up and down through the phone, bobbin unwinding to the spool,
your fingertips touching thread, guiding
the tension, foot pad on the foot control.
      The throat plate patter-thud presses

up, down, back and forth.

The bodice on your cranberry dress is tough
        to sew, the throat plate shimmies back and forth
like a tongue, *la la, hush, la la, hush, hush,*
the way the rose garden greeted us in Balboa Park,
        where you and I found ourselves full-bloomed
pink petals drifting on the lily pond.
Monsoons break open in autumn now, flood
        everything, blood-red leaves from the dogwood
drown, cream-colored buds will hold up the frost
like tranquil flames, poised for their lush rebirth.
        Didn't we stroke angel wings once
in the snow with our limbs, like a fire
waving from earth, then a naked patch signaling
        Over here, floating and bare, *here we are.*

Robin Carstensen's chapbook *In the Temple of Shining Mercy* is the recipient of an annual first-place award by Iron Horse Literary Press and was published in 2017. Poems also appear in *BorderSenses, Southern Humanities Review, Voices de La Luna,* Demeter Press's anthology, *Borderlands and Crossroads: Writing the Motherland,* and many more. She directs the creative writing program at Texas A&M University-CC where she advises *The Windward Review: literary journal of the South Texas Coastal Bend,* and is co-founding, senior editor for the *Switchgrass Review.*

Singer

Jan Chronister

It holds the power
of Edison
under its arm.
Full of faith in machinery
I press the pedal,
thread from spool and bobbin
loop, smooth stitches form.

Magic flows out
despite thick fabric
dull needles.
Flat pieces of cloth
become full-blown gowns
like Cinderella's in the movie
I watched as a child.

Whir of the motor
hypnotizes me
invokes my mother
who sat in this chair for hours
full of hope and dreams.

If only I could sew a door
for the dead so she could
step through to me
and sing.

Jan Chronister lives and writes in the woods near Maple, Wisconsin. Her poems have appeared in *Rat's Ass Review, OVS Magazine, Weatherbeaten Lit, The Great Gatsby Anthology* and others. Her chapbook *Target Practice* was published by Parallel Press at the University of Wisconsin in 2009 and a full-length poetry collection *Caught between Coasts* was released by Clover Valley Press in 2018. Jan currently serves as president of the Wisconsin Fellowship of Poets. More about her work:www.janchronisterpoetry.wordpress.com.

Our Great Grandmothers

Magdalene Fry

were sewing trees into
the fingers of long
clouds,

to us they looked,
saying, give us a hand.

we clapped
until it was dark
all over.

Magdalene Fry is a single parent poet from Wayne County, West Virginia, and no longer resides in Appalachia. She studied Philosophy and Literary Theory at Anglia Ruskin and Marshall University.

Gina 1: 22 Ballard Avenue

Kelly Fordon

After the funeral, I had a dream. You were sitting in a field of buttercups. You said, "Tell them I'm happy now." Funny. I thought you were happy, neighbor. You lived in a gingerbread house. During the night, you painted your daughter's bathroom Barbie pink. You worked out. You ate organic. At night, we drank multi-colored margaritas and laughed. There were babies involved but we tried not to let them get to us. Who has not had to beat their demon back with a large broom? I thought you had a handle on him. Your skin was better than mine. You were younger. You earned real money. I should have known something was wrong when I met your parents, American Gothic. When the phone call came, I knew what had happened before the words reached me. Why was that? After the dream, I googled yellow flowers. They weren't buttercups after all.

Kelly Fordon's work has appeared in *The Florida Review, The Kenyon Review (KRO), Rattle* and various other journals. Her novel-in-stories, *Garden for the Blind,* was chosen as a 2016 Michigan Notable Book among other awards. *On the Street Where We Live,* a one-act play adapted from her poetry, was chosen for the 2018 Dream Up Festival in New York. She is the author of three award-winning poetry chapbooks and a full-length poetry collection, *Goodbye Toothless House* (2019). Another full-length poetry collection *SNAP* will be published in 2020. www.kellyfordon.com.

Horticulture

Mary Bamburg

I. Delusions

Blue hydrangeas in my backyard
yesterday insisted
they were pink.

A surgical snip-snip
and I set them in front of the mirror
to see for themselves.

II. Nomenclature

The hyacinth girl,
you always wanted us to call you —
innocent bright-eyed victim,
arms full of petals.

Really you were just trying to hide
those shining shears
long as your forearm
before anyone noticed the bloody stems.

III. Conceit

There is a rose
curled
tightly in my throat.
Petal by petal,
it unfurls.

I hold my peace,
or the blossom holds it for me.

I inhale summer nectar;

crimson smears down my throat.
I am eight petals away
from a voice.

Mary Bamburg is a South Louisiana poet who teaches high school English and spends too much time by the river. Her poetry has appeared in *Cordite Poetry Review*, *Belle Rêve Literary Journal*, *The Gambler Mag*, *From the Roaring Deep*, *Tracks*, and *With Lyre and Bow*.

Still Life with Apples & a Cup of Tea

Stella Vinitchi Radulescu

I talk to you from my bed hanging
from the ceiling hanging
from a dream

my grandmother smiles from
her framed picture
next to the book open at page twenty five

where somebody wrote a poem

still life with apples...

or maybe he didn't even write it
& ate the apples & drank
the tea

the yellow cup & the knife in the kitchen
pierce the eye

in front of me   infinity   a thought
looking for a place to settle down

today is gone & yesterday again

I am thirsty I am sad   the day lingers
on the couch
the hallway then   ends in the garden

I hear a step   a noise   & I think of you
living with the stars.

Stella Vinitchi Radulescu, Ph.D. in French Language & Literature, is the author of several collections of poetry published in the United States, Romania and France. She writes poetry in English, French and Romanian and her poems have appeared in *Asheville Poetry Review, Pleiades, Louisville Review, Laurel Review, Rhino, Wallace Stevens Journal, Seneca Review* among others, as well as in a variety of literary magazines in France, Belgium, Luxembourg, and Romania. Her last collection of poetry *I scrape the window of nothingness - new & selected poems* was released in 2015 from Orison Books Press. At the present she lives in Chicago.

Antenatal Classes

Kelly Dolejsi

There are seven new stars born
each year in our galaxy. I don't
even know how I like
my hair. Why bother to imagine
these rotating gas beads

or the vastness of the womb?
A religious search, I guess, a plea
for the exquisite. I rub the rag
along the top of the DVD player
and shake the new nebula

with the rest into the backyard
among the ant hills, the swingset,
the peony bush that looks like sticks,
or claws, or scratches in the day,
today a solid, damaged form,

but still, a star might gestate
for millions of years in its cloud
of dust and clumps. My fingers
clutch at my cloud of hair
beneath the cloudless sky.

Kelly Dolejsi's work has been published in *Cincinnati Review*, *North American Review*, *Denver Quarterly*, *Fifth Wednesday*, *Under a Warm Green Linden*, *Landfill*, and *Metafore*, among other journals. Her poem "Loyalty" was nominated for the Best of the Net in 2017. Her chapbook, *That Second Starling*, was published by Desert Willow Press in 2018. A graduate of Emerson College in Boston, she now lives in Los Alamos, NM.

The Fates Hang Wallpaper

Elizabeth Vignali

We furl and uncurl, dip and brush. We cut. We align
paper roses seam to seam, pink petals lipped edge
to edge, shadow to shadow, light to light. Leaf
leaps to leaf across invisible crevices. We unspool
paper in whispering strips. We slacken, we straighten.
We cut. If we do our job right (and we always do),
you'll never know it could have been otherwise.
Leaf might have given way to rose, petal to thorn,
stem to sky. Atropos unrolls the length of paper.
Clotho lacquers the wall with acrid glue. Lachesis
shears it off. Even we have our small rebellions.

Elizabeth Vignali is an optician and writer in the Pacific Northwest, where she coproduces the Bellingham Kitchen Sessions reading series. She is the author of *Object Permanence* and coauthor of *Your Body A Bullet*. Her poems and essays have appeared in *Willow Springs, Cincinnati Review, Mid-American Review, Timber, Tinderbox, The Literary Review,* and elsewhere.

Still Life With Fruit, Froth, & Kinesis

Jacquelyn Shah

On a rosewood dining room table overflowing a lead-crystal bowl: apple
kiwi lemon guava   cantaloupe sloped over grapefruit pissing off peach &
pear
papaya   breadfruit starfruit jackfruit   date & durian   apricot banding with
kumquat nectarine mango tangelo lime pineapple pumpkin chin-upping
cherries
berries black & blue   & dew huckle goose elder   rasp & straw & cran &
bil
lichee licking a quince   grapes all peeled black-red-green   champagne &
globe
honeydew water & crashaw melons   persimmon & plum perfecting
themselves
tangerine plantain coconut currants oranges, copious mandarin navel &
blood
seeds squealing out from a fat pomegranate as raisins debate &debate the
dubious
wonders of botox   figs & bananas bananas bananas-of-course   a little green
worm is fucking the fruit— apple   then kiwi   lemon   guava . . . all in the
fog
of a grand starbuckian steamed-milk froth . . .

Jacquelyn "Jacsun" Shah is drawn to quirky / absurdist / surrealist works.
Founder of protest organization Women Against Violence Everywhere (now
defunct) and founding member of Voices Breaking Boundaries, a literary arts
organization, she has taught creative writing through WITS (Writers In The
Schools) and the University of Houston, where she completed both M.F.A. and
Ph.D. in creative writing. She has received grants from the Houston Arts
Alliance, published poems in journals, published a chapbook, *small fry*
(Finishing Line Press), and published a full-length book, *What to Do with Red*
(Lit Fest Press).

Intoxication

Claire Ibarra

My mother drapes herself in lace like Queen Elizabeth. She wears wigs. Her favorites are the Cher (long, iron-straight black), the Bonnie Raitt (red goes with her leopard print jumpsuit), and the Marie Antoinette (crimped, platinum blonde she wears with satin). She likes costumes: the southern belle, the voodoo priestess, the Stevie Nicks rock star. I've seen the pictures.

My mother is a hoarder, living in a genie's bottle. She is a painter, a cabaret singer, and a dressmaker. She paints pictures of girls holding flowers, ballerinas, and bridesmaids cloaked in the dresses she makes, in a yellow the color of bile.

My mother tells me I'm an octopus. I am purple with spots, and innocuous. My mother becomes lost in my sea. I discover she is housed within a submarine barrack. I come upon great iron doors with padlocks; a submerged prison; an inferno without fire. Hades is an ocean, an Everest of pressure and tidal forces. My efforts to save her are futile.

My mother is locked away for seducing my daughters with ideas of lace and wigs, precious rings on every manicured finger, wine and sweets to make us plump and intoxicated with a sleepy, dreary bliss: the very bliss that drugs us into submission.

Claire Ibarra received her MFA in creative writing from Florida International University. Her poetry has appeared in many literary journals and anthologies, including *Origins, The Midwest Quarterly, Pirene's Fountain, Thrush Poetry Journal*, and *Literary Orphans*. Claire's poetry chapbook is *Vortex of Our Affections*, published by Finishing Line Press in 2017. Claire enjoys photography, teaching, and traveling.

My Anguished Goulash

Lana Bella

The speed of my earthy hunger,
with all its leaf to bud to stem,
asked for my anguished goulash
of garlic broth and the dark-
ripening of molasses' granular
prismatic. I was here as the dust-
grey of night's end trayveled with
my fingertips through vats of
goosefat and jars of custard on
the shelf, down to the steep place
where a trail of spice whetted its
blade above the swill of my vodka.
Liquefying myself to the cabbage
and meats screaming in the crock,
I thought of the mingling salt of
Egg Benedict and strips of bacon
curling to the iconic sadness lying
just a little too close to my heart.

A four-time Pushcart Prize, five-time *Best of the Net*, & *Bettering American Poetry* nominee, **Lana Bella** is an author of three chapbooks, *Under My Dark* (Crisis Chronicles Press), *Adagio* (Finishing Line Press), and *Dear Suki: Letters* (Platypus 2412 Mini Chapbook Series), has work featured in over 520 journals, *The Cortland Review*, *EVENT*, *The Fortnightly Review*, *Ilanot Review*, *Midwest Quarterly*, *New Reader*, *Notre Dame Review*, *Sundress Publications*, & *Whiskey Island*, among others, and *Aeolian Harp Anthology, Volume 3*. Lana resides in the US and the coastal town of Nha Trang, Vietnam, where she is a mom of two far-too-clever frolicsome imps.

Home Remedy

Ellen Estilai

Wild rue scattered on smoldering embers,
acrid smoke rising, swirling,
finding its way to the back of the throat;
pails of water chasing fragrant ghosts of dust from stones;
the perfume of a lump of opium,
reduced by charcoal to burnt syrup.

Preserve these memories in syrup.
Concentrate them in a clay pot set in embers
until they become the color of opium.
Chased by a wooden spoon, swirling,
spinning, they become like amber, the precious stones
an old lady hangs below her sagging throat.

When the rasp of regret coats your throat,
drink this syrup,
walk barefoot on cool stones,
fill a censer with embers
and wild rue and swing it, swirling
smoke more potent than opium.

An old man sits cross-legged at his brazier, preparing his opium.
He sighs, eyes closed, and clears his throat.
His daughters circle him, their red skirts swirling,
their fears thicker than syrup,
their desires redder than embers,
their despair dumber than stones.

The daughters fill their mouths with stones.
The old man savors his opium.
The daughters walk on embers.
The smoke fills the old man's throat.
The daughters turn to syrup.

The old man remembers red skirts, swirling.

Fragrant ghosts of dust swirling,
thought-dervishes spinning on hot stones,
blood turning to syrup,
the old man is left with a lump of burnt opium.
A cry sticks in his throat:
I still see you in the embers.

Wild rue dispatches the evil eye—not opium.
It catches your enemy by the throat,
reducing his envy to embers.

Ellen Estilai, formerly executive director of the Riverside Arts Council and the Arts Council for San Bernardino County, has taught in universities in Iran and California. Her essay "Front Yard Fruit," originally published in *Alimentum*, is included in *New California Writing 2011* and was selected as a notable essay in *The Best American Essays 2011*. A Pushcart and Orison prize nominee, she has published in *Phantom Seed, Broad!, Snapdragon, Ink & Letters, Heron Tree, (In)Visible Memoirs 2, HOME: Tall Grass Writers Guild Anthology, Shark Reef,* and *Riddled with Arrows*, among others. Ellen is a founding board member and past-president of the Inlandia Institute, a literary center and publishing house based in Riverside, California.

Feng Shui

Kristin Camitta Zimet

We lie down with our feet to grandma's lamp.
One hangdog bulb hiccups and passes out.
Beside it, on the desk, my yellowlegs
wades up to its carved belly in a bog
of bills. A clock staggers in three-inch
matchstick numerals; they crook a curve,
fizzling as we squint. Something is
stuck back of the drawers: they spit
socks at us; they cannot quite shut up.
Under the chair, in limbo, mill
our piled mementos, which exude
a rhubarb buzz of extras hanging out
at central casting. Facing these,
we mean to sleep, to love?

Kristin Camitta Zimet is the author of *Take in My Arms the Dark* (a full length collection of poetry) and the editor of *The Sow's Ear Poetry Review*. Her poetry is in journals including *Salamander*, *Natural Bridge*, and *Poet Lore*, and in a great many anthologies. She co-founded a small troupe of actors who perform poetry theater.

The Thirst of the Prior Inhabitants

Annah Browning

When we were alive, there was a lake.
There was a lake and it was summer.
The house was already an oddness,

an edifice. And we felt perfectly
inside it, perfectly safe. The gnaws
in the walls were gnaws that were

known, so they were safe. Yet mice
are combatants, much as the ground is.
We talked of damp as something

that rose. We rose and walked many
days to the end of the road, fluttering
coats, and willed the mail to come.

We ignored the moistness in our armpits,
the humid attire of the crotch. We
ignored our mouths, our constant

swallow, the wetness of the forks
on our plates, the end of the meal.
We rose and went to bed. We went

to bed and rose. We glow pink
and soft as roses now. Though
you can barely see us, I suppose.

How winter it is, how quiet. Here
with you, watching you open
your wet little mouth.

Annah Browning is the author of *Witch Doctrine*, a 2018 Editor's Choice selection in the Akron Series in Poetry, forthcoming from University of Akron Press, as well as a chapbook, *The Marriage*, (Horse Less Press). She is also poetry editor and cofounder of *Grimoire Magazine*. Her poetry has appeared in *Indiana Review*, *Willow Springs*, *Boulevard*, and *elsewhere*, and a narrative horror video game she illustrated and co-wrote, titled *Heloise & Wulf*, was published by Black Warrior Review Online. She holds an MFA from Washington University in St. Louis and a PhD from the University of Illinois at Chicago. While she hails from the foothills of South Carolina, she currently calls Chicago home, where she is a visiting lecturer in English and a faculty member of the Honors College at the University of Illinois at Chicago.

Why I Have Five Calendars in My Kitchen

Hilary King

One is a window. Through it I watch
our days grow tall and thick.

One is a sky. Tiny numbers form constellations.
A belt, a ladle, a vacation in July.

One is a poker hand. I call, I raise, I fold.
Time is a cheater. The house never wins.

One hangs high on stainless steel.
Beneath it hang ideas, directions, a red paper heart.

One is a campfire. Each night we warm ourselves
by the sight of last year's Easter, last year's beach trip,
our own happy faces flickering in the past.

Hilary King is a poet and playwright living in the Bay Area of Northern
California. She is the author of the book of poems *The Maid's Car.*

Cook

Akua Lezli Hope

She must crack
this hard perfection
rap it sideways
on tempered glass edge
hold its brimming viscous clarity
above the waiting whisk
pour from one fractured cup
to other

Jagged teeth strain
what will foam
from what will thicken

Blood spot stains
butter-orb's glisten

In this space
between eternities
known and unknown —
outside where orbs bounce
and seeds break
through earth into spears
on which her children dance or trammel
inside where digits jitter
and debts mount as ice melts
in alcohol like polar caps
in carbon warmed seas

Can she earn what this
shattering may yield,
will flan, waffle, pancake
meet the glory
that was unbroken
ovum.

Akua Lezli Hope, a third-generation New Yorker, is a creator who uses sound, words, fiber, glass, metal, and wire to create poems, patterns, stories, music, ornaments, adornments and peace whenever possible. Her awards include two Artists Fellowships from the New York Foundation for the Arts, a Ragdale U.S.-Africa Fellowship, a Creative Writing Fellowship from The National Endowment for The Arts and the Walker Foundation Scholarship to Provincetown Fine Arts Work Center, among others. She is a Cave Canem fellow. In 2017 she was a Rhysling award finalist. Two of her poems are nominated for the 2018 Pushcart Prize. *Them Gone*, her poetry collection, was published by The Word Works Press in 2018. Her first collection, *Embouchure*, Poems on Jazz and Other Musics, won a Writer's Digest book award for poetry. She has twice won Rattle's Poets Respond. Akua has given hundreds of readings and founded a paratransit nonprofit so that folks like her could get around her small upstate New York town.

History's Private Life

Nandini Dhar

Outside, on the porch, Grandmother is sweeping
the glass shards off the floor. In this home, history

is never too far away. We children read her moving
lips: as if a blind woman touching her alphabets.

Neither me nor my sister broke the bottle. She
knows--yet thwacks us on the heads, a light

tap with her knuckles. Collects the shards, hides
them in the crevices of her comb. Oil-stains

on the mirror on the mantelpiece: hazy faces,
hazy names, hazy maps, hazy villages.

Inside, on the kitchen table, Mother
is carving glass shards into curse words. We know,

we cannot trust the castles. My sister says,
the bigger the castle the deeper the dungeon.

But, what we do not have is a history
of pushing soaps inside little girl mouths.

Mother tells us a story: the story of a little
girl hungry, in a very literal way. The story

of a little girl who learnt to suck milk
out of pebbles, apple-juice from sand, mango

pulp out of the scar on her brother's palm.
We suspect, the little girl is no one but our mother.

In the attic, the woman who hides her sorrow
in a jewelry box, is teaching our youngest aunt

the shortest and the most efficient ways
of transmutating to Thumbelina.

Nandini Dhar is the author of the chapbook *Lullabies Are Barbed Wire Nations* (Two of Cups Press). Her poems have recently appeared or are forthcoming in *The Chattahoochee Review, Grist, Tusculum Review, West Branch*, and elsewhere. She is the co-editor of the journals *Elsewhere* and *Aainanagar*. Nandini hails from Kolkata, India, and divides her time between her hometown and Miami, Florida, where she currently works as an Assistant Professor of English at Florida International University.

Overly Melodramatic Waltz
with Goldfish

Kelli Russell Agodon

Any sort of happiness has never much interested me,
instead I'm a sucker for sadness, for the sorrow
of bones and the songs that make spoiled men cry,

and when I say *spoiled*, I don't mean *having too much*,
but as in *gone bad*, the way you find a forgotten
lemon at the bottom of a bowl and a cloud of fruit flies

follows. These are the sad songs I shoulder, the cracked
dish in the kitchen, the diabetic cat licking the frosting
of the cake someone left out. We know he won't live

as long as we hope, nor will the chunky golden retriever
whose hips ache, whose back legs are beginning
to fail. Sing me your weepy melodies, your muddled

crossword puzzles, the arguments you lost
as I meandered through my tangledness
under a chipped sky. I'm the seasick goldfish

in a tank of tears—yes, it's that bad, Captain Ahab,
that low, Sailor Noah. Let me ring out your rainbow,
as the situation's grave, a depression of poets,

an exaggeration of catastrophes. We are a dismal dance
in a wet world, our hands open and clinging
to each other and a soggy olive branch darting through

this broken ceramic castle in which we hide.

Kelli Russell Agodon is a poet, writer, and editor from the Pacific Northwest. She is the author of six books, most recently, *Hourglass Museum* (Finalist for the Washington State Book Prize and shortlisted for the Julie Suk Prize), *The Daily Poet: Day-By-Day Prompts For Your Writing Practice,* and *Letters from the Emily Dickinson Room,* winner of ForeWord Magazine's Book of the Year in Poetry. Kelli is the cofounder of Two Sylvias Press where she works as an editor and book cover designer. Her work has appeared in magazines such as *The Atlantic, O, The Oprah Magazine,* and *Prairie Schooner.* She lives in a sleepy seaside town where when not writing, she's an avid paddleboarder, hiker, and beachcomber. She recently learned how to properly cut a pineapple. Visit her at www.agodon.com and www.twosylviaspress.com

We Appreciate Your Comments and Suggestions!

Martha Silano

If you're impressed with the way we've rigged the fish tank
with a spooky chartreuse pagoda, a scuba diving fella

with algal accents, please advise. If the receptionist opened
her mouth not unlike a submerged gnome, belted out her best

Howard Dean scream as she handed you the questionnaire,
we'd like to know. Were you satisfied with the level of spice

in the blood pressure ball, or do you favor five alarm?
Should we bulldoze the waiting room BBQ shack,

replace it with a sushi bar? Did the deeply pleated,
sand-papery hospital gowns meet your needs,

or did our attempt at providing modesty when you're
spread-eagled like a pullet elicit tears? If you were, like,

what's up with the retro pseudo-leather couch,
we're all ears. Isn't it great when a waiting room

doesn't smell like clove oil, cat piss, last night's rabbit stew?
If you concur, please let us know. You have to admit

the sequined latex gloves add a festive touch. And how about
those faux-fur mini blinds? Always happy to serve you

as you check the boxes for irritable bowel syndrome, jaw pain, boils.
We value your willingness to engage in an active dialogue

with our idea management system; as a token of thanks,
please retrieve your urine sample as you exit.

Martha Silano's books include *Gravity Assist*, *Reckless Lovely*, and *The Little Office of the Immaculate Conception* (all from Saturnalia Books). She also co-edited, with Kelli Russell Agodon, *The Daily Poet: Day-By-Day Prompts For Your Writing Practice*. Martha's poems have appeared in *Poetry*, *Paris Review*, *American Poetry Review*, and elsewhere. She teaches at Bellevue College.

Trade

Jackie Sherbow

You were a carpenter
in my memory
but now I see that I have
confused you with something
else I hold the drawer

that has fallen out
of the table next to the bed
          you are making words
          out of white magnets on
          the white refrigerator you
          spell *you are* and *you are not*
                    I have been standing here
                    for so long I wonder
                    if I have become the table
                    next to the bed it is cold

                    in the kitchen the window
                    is open you are standing

                    with one foot resting against
                    your other foot you've opened
                    the refrigerator inside it
                    dark spots have gathered

                    in all the corners you notice
                    me staring tell me
                    you cannot fix
                    the drawer
                    (you didn't
                    make it)

I want to tie your fingers
together with thin plastic wire

knotting it on either side
of each knuckle (like a craft)
                        you say you understand
                        but you don't you spell
                        and yet still with magnets
                        on the refrigerator

                                        I say I understand but I don't
                                        I tie my hands with fishing line
                                        I shake my head back and forth
                                        until my hair covers my eyes

I thought you were a fisherman
but you don't know what
to do with these tiny metal
lures they are supposed
to look like rain and the way
you have made them they

look like coins and they fill
the drawer in the table next
to the bed they spill onto
the floor you untie me say

                        *look what you
                        have done* I do not move
                        please

                        close the window close
                        the refrigerator door
                        it's freezing in here.

Jackie Sherbow is a writer and editor living in Queens, NY. Her poems have appeared or are forthcoming in *Coffin Bell*, *Okay Donkey*, *Moonchild Magazine*, *Bad Pony*, *Day One*, and elsewhere, and have been part of the Emotive Fruition performance series. She works as an editor for two leading mystery-fiction magazines as well as Newtown Literary, the literary journal dedicated to the borough of Queens.

Last House Screen Door

Sarah Ann Winn

> *The last house on the northern end of Holland Island*
> *has fallen into the Chesapeake Bay.*

Kim Hairston, "Chesapeake Bay Island Vanishes."
Baltimore Sun, October 21, 2010

That first night, I dove in dreams to the last house on Holland Island, fallen into the bay. I flashlit my way down, drifted by the kitchen door, which stood ajar. Through the screen, I saw how everything settled. The refrigerator slid forward as the house fell, carving tracks in the wood floor, and the scrapes are freshest looking thing in the whole kitchen. The museum magnet pattern remains intact, Magritte's apple blocking my first-grade face, hatless. Klimt's lovers embrace in celebration of your math quiz results, 98% still a victory, even twenty years gone.

Everything wavers.

Even the old-fashioned refrigerator cord, ripped from the wall during descent, still frizzes — snapped and frayed. Left raw, its split ends splay towards the sink.

Somehow the cake stand survived the tumble. It rests in the middle of the floor — milk glass tiers, intricate as a coral reef, basket woven. We celebrated with it every year.

I couldn't bring myself to go in.

Sarah Ann Winn's first book, *Alma Almanac*, was selected by Elaine Equi as winner of the 2017 Barrow Street Book Prize. She's the author of five chapbooks, the most recent of which, *Ever After the End Matter*, is forthcoming from Porkbelly Press in 2019. She teaches poetry workshops in Northern Virginia and the DC Metro area, and online at the Loft Literary Center. Visit her at http://bluebirdwords.com or follow her @blueaisling.

The Mermaid of California

Melinda Palacio

All that ocean   don't drink the water.

My grandmother says it straight, I don't like water.
We drink Coca Cola instead. She put Coke in my baby bottle.

Oceans gush oil, Pacific and the Gulf of Mexico.
All that ocean   don't drink the water.

Orleans Parish, St. Bernard and Jefferson warn against brain
eating amoebas in New Orleans tap water. The world has never been safe.

As a child growing up in Los Angeles, I loved going to the beach.
What's not to love?

Ocean water crashes, then dies to a whisper of sea foam. She is a show-off
as she twists, turns, and takes. The ocean does not wait for God's approval.

Seagulls squawk as the birds circle for food and treasure.
Kids taunt waves with the their cherub feet as a familiar song
plays softly from a sun-soaked girl's radio.

The bronze girl doesn't care if her mother warned of water pollution
at the beach. She swims on a dare, ringlets past her shoulders and bikini
strings bounce. Water tickles her feet, and she morphs into a mermaid.

All that ocean   Mermaid, don't drink the water.

Melinda Palacio is a poet, author, and speaker. She lives in Santa Barbara and New Orleans. Her poetry chapbook, *Folsom Lockdown*, won Kulupi Press' Sense of Place 2009 award. She is the author of the novel, *Ocotillo Dreams* (ASU Bilingual Press), for which she received the Mariposa Award for Best First Book at the 2012 International Latino Book Awards and a 2012 PEN Oakland-Josephine Miles Award for Excellence in Literature. Her first full-length poetry collection, *How Fire Is a Story, Waiting*, (Tia Chucha Press) was a finalist for the Milt Kessler Award, the Paterson Prize, and received First Prize in Poetry at the 2013 International Latino Book Awards. Melinda's new poetry collection, *Bird Forgiveness*, was published by 3Taos Press in 2018.

If the ocean had a mouth

Marie-Elizabeth Mali

I'd lean close, my ear
to her whisper and roar,
her tongue scattered
with stars.

She'd belt her brassy voice
over the waves' backbeat.
No one sings better than her.

Would she ever bite
the inside of her cheek?

Would she yell at the moon
to quit tugging at her hem,
or would she whistle, drop
her blue dress and shimmy
through space to cleave
to that shimmer?

What did she mean to say
that morning she spit out
the emaciated whale
wearing a net for a corset?

All this emptying
on the sand. Eyeless
shrimp. Oiled pelicans.

Within her jaws the coral forests,
glittering fish, waves like teeth,
her hungry mortal brine.

Marie-Elizabeth Mali is the author of *Steady, My Gaze* (Tebot Bach) and co-editor with Annie Finch of the anthology, *Villanelles* (Everyman's Library Pocket Poets). Her work has appeared in *New Ohio Review*, *Poet Lore*, and *RATTLE*, among others. As a Midlife Transformation Specialist, she guides women over 40 to give themselves permission to want what they want and create a life that reflects the truth of who they are. You can learn more and read more of her work at www.memali.com.

She Opened Walls

Ingrid Jendrzejewski

Mar her into
other angles:
her abandonment
seemed
the world or
rhythm
of pain.
She opened
walls.

Her body gave
the house
a flesh:
growth,
wonder,
more rooms
and windows,
clothes.

Left by limping,
angular notions
of her light,
she took
the side of
irritation
from within
pink wallpaper.

Before the surface
of night
crawled out
from the tearing,
she,

like a pearl,
fell:
days
collapsed.

Source: All words in this poem appeared on page 108 of the following text: Sexson, Lynda. Margaret of the Imperfections: stories. New York: Persea Books, 1988. 108. Print.

Ingrid Jendrzejewski grew up in Vincennes, Indiana, studied creative writing at the University of Evansville, then physics at the University of Cambridge. Her work has found homes in places like *Passages North, Rattle, The Los Angeles Review, The Conium Review, The Mainichi,* and *The Liars' League* (London & NYC). Links to Ingrid's work can be found at www.ingridj.com and she occasionally tweets @LunchOnTuesday. When not writing, Ingrid enjoys cryptic crosswords, the python programming language and the game of Go.

Plumb

Nora Boxer

So this is the floor.

Persephone once,
in another decade,
dove through the tiles,
left a pomegranate atop the blue-and-white checkers,

laid out a single souvenir:
language as the underworld of the heart.

Now she wakes
to chimes and routines,
the muteness of a mountain,
chattering conjugations of a retrieval gone wrong.

What kind of undoing is this, staged in the kitchen
the slope of the house where she knew it would all sink.

So this is the floor.

The floor under all the myths.
It's no longer bottomless.
It says, listen:

believe too much in language
and it will fail you, in attachment turn
from heart revolver,
from season-turner

to rotted fruit.

Poet and fiction writer **Nora Boxer** is a recipient of the Keene Prize for Literature. Her poems have appeared in *Catamaran Literary Reader, Spiral Orb, Pilgrimage, Prism Review, The Turnip Truck(s)* & others. She has been a writer/artist in residence at the Byrdcliffe Arts Colony, the Elsewhere Collaborative, Maumauworks Istanbul, and The Art Monastery Project. Nora holds an MA in fiction from UT Austin and teaches creative writing at SF City College. Visit her at www.noraboxer.com.

The Minotaur

Jade Hurter

When I was born I cracked my mother to the sternum. She bled for days, and when they sewed her up she was never the same, said Father: a woman cut in half, though she'd always been a woman divided. I suckled until she cut me off, with blades fit against her nipples. My sliced mouth dripped over the breakfast table, rust in the milky tea, I couldn't hold my fork for shaking. When I got older I didn't fit on the bus, so I walked to school, clip-clopping along the pavement. The kids all liked my hooves, but they never asked me over for birthday cake or pool parties. Father would watch me do homework in the afternoons, his eyes dark slits. I cried when Mother was at work, cried when she came home and smacked the tough hide of my backside. You're a monster, she told me. Act like it. When other children turned thirteen, their parents threw them parties at the roller rink. I heard them talking about it in the cafeteria, but of course no one made skates for feet like mine. I turned thirteen and Mother put me out of the house. She left me to sleep in the garden, to eat the scraps of toast and orange peel Father left on the windowsill each evening. I got used to it. The crickets, the jays, the passionvine that twisted around my horns as I slept. I picked caterpillars off the sweet olive, grew dizzy with the smell of orange blossom. Soon I began to pull out the weeds, to clip the rosebushes into hedges, until I had fashioned a verdant maze. In the center, it was so quiet. I only wanted to be alone.

Jade Hurter is the author of the chapbook *Slut Songs* (Hyacinth Girl Press), and her work has appeared in *THRUSH, The Columbia Poetry Review, Glass, Passages North, New South,* and elsewhere. She teaches English at the University of New Orleans.

Until I Wasn't

Jen Rouse

In my head I am very small,
ducking under dewy leaves
adorned with strawberry blossoms
aching in white with crisp yellow centers.
All of my houses are miniature, and, even
my home, where no one lives anymore
but the dust ghosts, small orbs
of light and sometimes laughter,
was thimble-sized. We grew a bottle
garden. Tiny vials that sprung up
singing, "Drink me!" And the ones
that tasted like lavender
made us forget. And the ones
that glistened like ripe cherries
on your lips, I want to forget.
On the corner of nostalgia
and regret, I left a giant
leather boot, one you had
loaned me. A whole family
lives there now. Here the sun sets
like a lemon drop and sounds like
a Clapton medley. You wanted
the whole world to see you,
as vast as galaxies. I watched
until I wasn't.

Jen Rouse is the Director of the Center for Teaching and Learning at Cornell College in Mount Vernon, IA. She is a two-time finalist for the Charlotte Mew Prize with Headmistress Press, and her most recent collection is entitled *CAKE*. Her chapbook *Riding with Anne Sexton* was recently reissued by Headmistress Press.

Capricornucopia (The Dream of the Goats)

paulA neves

Goats appeared at the door,
asking to eat the house from inside out.
It was Christmas, so we let them enter.
The drink-laden guests parted.

Sure footed on the walnut-inlaid parquet,
the beasts made for the manger first,
ate the fake hay with unbridled relish.

The billygoat then eyed the end tables
my girlfriends and I had saved from curbs
and I had carried on my back
to whatever places we were calling home.

All the females followed billyboy's suit—
whatever they're called, girlygoats?
I know what they are but regardless

everyone looked at me as if the goats
could see through walls—
an insight out of Freud or Foucault.
My new girlfriend looked pissed.

The goats made for the sofa.
"Who are they to you?" My girlfriend insisted.
Stuffing fell about us like snow.

The billygoat toppled the tree.
Blown glass ornaments blew everywhere.

Some shattered. Some dangled
from his horns like disco earrings.

"Androgyny went out in the 80's,
when you were still young,"
I heard at my ear.

I hoped it was the voice of the devil
I didn't know—a future lover perhaps,
her flutes as piercing, her heart as cloven
as any Pan I could ask for (and have).

But it was only my mother,
who whispered, "Did you ever
turn on the oven?"
Then added, "You're starting to get whiskers,
just like them."
Tender, the words went through me like a horn.

Mercifully, someone shouted, "They're headed for the table!"
And so the goats were. Like midnight buffet tourists,
they charged the sweetmeats, the Mouton Cadet,
the *chanfana*[*] like grandma used to make.

"Cannibalism. At Christmas no less,"
a faceless relative
tsk tsk'ed.

Let them.
Let them be goats.
Let them eat everything—

                         even the bones.

* *traditional Portuguese goat or mutton dish stewed in wine in the oven.*

paulA neves is a Luso-American writer, mixed media artist, and Newark native who plans on playing recreational soccer well into dotage. neves, whose work often considers, overtly or otherwise, the legacies of immigrant forebears (including love of said soccer) is the author of the chapbook *capricornucopia: the dream of the goats* (Finishing Line Press) and the co-author, with photographer Nick Kline, of the poetry/photography collection *Shirts & Skins* (Shine Portrait Studio Press). Other writing has appeared in *Pittsburg Poetry Houses, Newest Americans, The Acentos Review, Cleaver Magazine, Queen Mob's Teahouse*, Writers of the Portuguese Diaspora, and elsewhere. neves teaches for various programs at Rutgers University, was a teaching artist-in-residence for the GlassBook Project, and has exhibited mixed media works in several of its collections and other gallery shows. neves holds an MFA in poetry from Rutgers-Newark. Visit paulaneves.net or @itinerantmuse for more.

Why Break into a Flock of Small Red Winter Birds When I Hand you the Green Clementine?

Jennifer Martelli

My own sin is easily lost in the sofa pillows with the old figs: I want
five of everything, five of your tears and five of the birds that flew out of your
hair.

Forgive me, the man you brought to my home
ate all the holiday food: the scar on his cheek could fit an apple seed.

I suggest you don't try the toddy or eggnog from the glass mugs,
don't drink anything. List your defects and pray they are blown up the flue.

Oh, it's easy to re-gift a fruitcake, try giving five golden ring
fingers of your man, try giving five ventricles, lung-colored ribs.

I'll take the dried cranberries wound around the Douglas fir, five blue lights,
the pentacle on the top of the tree.

Jennifer Martelli is the author of *My Tarantella* (Bordighera Press), as well as
the award-winning chapbook *After Bird* (Grey Book Press). Her work has
appeared or will appear in *Verse Daily, The Sonora Review, Iron Horse Review*
(winner, Photo Finish contest), *The Sycamore Review, Sugar House,
Superstition Review, Thrush,* and *Tinderbox Poetry Journal.* Her prose and
artwork have been published in *Five-2-One, The Baltimore Review,* and *Green
Mountains Review.* Jennifer Martelli has been nominated for Pushcart and Best
of the Net Prizes and is the recipient of the Massachusetts Cultural Council
Grant in Poetry. She is a poetry editor for *The Mom Egg Review.*

Tricks a Girl Can Do

Susan Rich

> *Hannah Maynard (1834-1918) was one of the first*
> *professional woman photographers in British*
> *Columbia; from 1884 to 1896 she created a series of*
> *proto-surreal self-portraits using multiple exposures*

I will hang myself in picture frames
in drawing rooms where grief
is not allowed a wicker chair

then grimace back at this facade
from umbrella eyes
through a lampshade of silvering hair.

Look! I've learned to slice myself in three
to sit politely at the table
with ginger punch and teacake;

offer thin-lipped graves
of pleasantries. I develop myself
in the pharmacist's chemicals

three women I'm loathe to understand—
presences I sometimes cajole
into porcelain light and shadow.

We culminate in a silver gelatin scene—
a daughter birthed from a spiral shell,
a keyhole tall enough to strut through.

Susan Rich is the author of five books including *Cloud Pharmacy, The Alchemist's Kitchen, Cures Include Travel*, and *The Cartographer's Tongue* (White Pine Press). She is co-editor of *The Strangest of Theatres: Poets Crossing Borders* (McSweeney's). Her poems have been published in *The Gettysburg Review, New England Review, Plume*, and *World Literature Today*. Recently, her work has been translated into Slovenian and Swedish.

Parable of the Lost Voice

Elizabeth S. Wolf

I cut the daisy from my throat.
Mute, I danced all I had to say,
flinging question marks and exclamation points
in bright droplets of blood.

I tore the signpost from my heart
and so lost my way. I plotted out all
possible courses, laid down a path,
bone by bone.

Silent and wandering
I discovered the world,
watered it with my tears.

Brambles sprouted, tangled and
prickly. By the second summer white
blossoms emerged, and then
black fleshy fruit, thick with juice.

At first, like the birds and
bears, I ate straight from the bush,
warily, clumsily, fighting with thorns.
But the sun-warmed berries nourished me
encouraged me
emboldened me.

Now I set a bowl on my own table,
settle with my bare feet resting on
well-worn ground. I am fed. I am home.

That's not the wind that you hear howling-
whispering roaring waning sighing-
That's me. I'm singing.

Elizabeth S. Wolf writes because telling stories is how we make sense of our world, how we heal, and how we celebrate. Elizabeth's poems have appeared in multiple anthologies & journals, including *Persian Sugar in English Tea* (in English and Farsi), *Mosaics: A Collection of Independent Women, Volume 1, The Best of Kindness: Origami Poems Project, Extreme: an anthology for social and environmental justice*, and *Scarlet Leaf Review*. Her chapbook *What I Learned: Poems* came out from Finishing Line Press in 2017. Her 2018 Rattle Chapbook Contest winner *Did You Know?* is forthcoming. Elizabeth lives in Massachusetts and works as a technical metadata librarian.

My tongue hatched; all at once

Melissa Atkinson Mercer

nothing I said made sense to anyone. I would try each truth three ways:
fog in the red mountain; my gateways accumulate; my name is ant.
I was daughter of the daughter of the woman who stole
every doorknob she could touch, glued them to her bed—the new bewilder,
the postern moon.
I would sew glass moths to my feet as she named them:
a sea-locked church; a mining town; a room of long candles.
Is this what life becomes? Cross-legged and quieted in the blood winter,
hearing my own stories told back to me.

Melissa Atkinson Mercer is the author of *Knock* (Half Mystic Press) and *Saint of the Partial Apology* (Five Oaks Press) as well as five poetry chapbooks, including *ghost exhibit* (Glass Poetry Press). Her work has recently appeared in *Moon City Review*, *Tinderbox Poetry Journal*, *Yes, Poetry*, and *A Portrait in Blues: An Anthology of Identity, Gender, and Bodies*, among others. She has an MFA from West Virginia University where she won the Russell MacDonald Creative Writing Award in Poetry.

Immaculate

Emily Vogel

The immaculate number descends from the dream of heaven and offers me the grace of a mother. Mother Mary, blue as any stone, cold as any early spring, freak snow of April, associate's heart. Mother Mary or myself, counting the fingers on my son's hand in the grocery line, while we buy milk, diapers, and Easter candy. Mother Mary sitting as some sort of poultry on a white cloud, cleaner than a generous face. Thought of a friend today and imagined the inky black of her hair, the naïve evening of her eyes. Thought of sending her a note, and then thought of the immaculate number. Thought of the inarticulate roar of cartoon tigers, real and perilous tigers, the stuffed tiger that my daughter holds close to her face to speak an ancient and alien language. Counted the immaculate number as I was getting my son ready for bed, changing him into his pajamas. Counted three cups of onions. The immaculate number is an inkling of pastel color in the sky. There might be too many onions. Counted the minute, Mother Mary like a phantom in a blue dress, knitting on the couch while the children play. My mother, throwing herself into any idea of an ocean, knitting, but with the knowledge of the hard reality and inevitability of earth. Mothers, in a bubble machine, testing the readiness of the walls, the stability of structures. Mothers, like idiomatic hearts. My daughter holds a Valentine's day balloon close to her face and speaks an alien language. All Mother appendages on deck. I hope there aren't too many onions in the meatloaf. Things recede and edge in like tides, like husbands leaving and returning home, only by the front door.

Emily Vogel's poetry, reviews, essays, and translations have most recently been published in *Omniverse, The North American Review, The Paterson Literary Review, Lips, City Lit Rag, Luna Luna, Maggy, Lyre Lyre,* and *PEN,* among several others. She is the author of five chapbooks, and a full-length collection, *The Philosopher's Wife,* published in 2011 by Chester River Press, a collaborative book of poetry, *West of Home,* with her husband Joe Weil (Blast Press), *First Words* (NYQ Books), and recently, *Dante's Unintended Flight* (NYQ Books). She has work forthcoming in *The Boston Review,* and *The Paterson Literary Review,* and in anthology on topics related to autism (NYQ Books). She has a children's book forthcoming *Clara's Song* (Swingin' Bridge Books). She teaches writing at SUNY Oneonta.

Venus de Milo Gets Ready
for the Halloween Party

Susan J. Erikson

The missing arms were a dead giveaway.
I'd need sleeves to cover youthful sins.
No way did I want to party talk with therapist types
about how I'd given my left arm
for love of some bozo whose helmet
glinted in the sun, shield held provocatively
to protect natural endowments.

Explaining the loss of the right was even more likely
to provoke, *How do you feel about that?*
Only the most beautiful of women believed
my answer: *I'd had it with the adoration bit.*
Drastic action was called for.

Witch, I thought as soon as I opened the invite.
Medusa, I decided after sleeping on the idea.
Medusa, too, had done a beauty-pedestal gig
until Athena got miffed, turned her tresses
to snakes and trashed her good looks—
making her sooo ugly anyone who looked into her
eyes turned to stone.

One night off from paragon-of-beauty duty,
I told myself as I dressed: black lipstick,
shades, atop my head a hundred writhing snakes
with glow-in-the-dark fangs, black gown with sleeves
flapping like wings of a vampire bat.

But habit hewn in marble is oh, so hard, to break.
I walked out the door, party bound,
one beautiful breast exposed.

Susan J. Erickson's book of poems in women's voices, *Lauren Bacall Shares a Limousine*, won the Brick Road Poetry Prize. Susan lives in Bellingham, Washington, where she helped establish the Sue C. Boynton Poetry Walk and Contest. Her poems appear in *Crab Creek Review, Rattle, Verse Daily, The Fourth River,* and *The Tishman Review*. Visit her at www.susanjerickson.

Robin

Mag Gabbert

The boys at school make fun of her—squawking,
flapping their arms like wings. They say her hair's
a tawny mess, a nest. By afternoon,
each amber curl is flecked with spitballs, white
and gray, a speckled feather-like display.
She folds paper while others play—a kite,
a crane with floral wings—then shuts her eyes
and dreams they fly away. Once home, she finds
the yard picked clean—no scattered peanuts left,
the crows already gone to nest. That night,
after she's tucked in bed, she sneaks back out
into the dark—too anxious now to rest,
she fumbles for the gifts they left: buttons,
a rusty nail, a heart-shaped zipper pull.

Mag Gabbert holds a PhD in creative writing from Texas Tech University and an MFA from The University of California at Riverside. Her essays and poems have been published in *32 Poems, Stirring, The Rumpus, The Boiler Journal, Whiskey Island, Phoebe, Anomaly, Carve Magazine*, and many other journals. Mag teaches creative writing for the Graduate Department of Liberal Studies at Southern Methodist University and for Writing Workshops Dallas; she serves as an associate editor for *Iron Horse Literary Review* and for *Underblong Journal*. For more information, please visit maggabbert.com.

Round Baby Absorbs Her Classmates

Sheila Squillante

Baby's getting rounder
by the day. Something growing
inside her. Someone starting
to make room. *You've got hips*
like battleships. An ass you could put
a map on. What? It's a compliment,
Baby! Bitch. Legs plush, belly billowing,
even her lips, that one boy said, *plump*
as pillows. Kissable and soft.
Baby has a choice to make: stuff this other
under peek-a-boo skin. Deny her girth, mirth.
Or, take all this delicious new
fat (ass) and fit it like a uniform,
let it (hips) squish against firm surfaces—
dressers, beds, the roof of the school &
other bolting bodies. Send it reeling, Baby;
set it loose and uncontained, bounding,
bouncing like a Super Ball, momentously
forward, a metaphor absorbing
your classmates, the school bus, the biting
boys, your neighbors, their houses,
sweet Sister, dim parents and the whole
round windowless world.

Sheila Squillante is the author of the collection *Beautiful Nerve* as well as several chapbooks. Her most recent series features an odd girl called Round Baby, who is mostly human, most of the time and who has recently been hanging around in places like *North Dakota Quarterly, Menacing Hedge* and *Rogue Agent*. She teaches in the MFA program at Chatham University in Pittsburgh where she edits *The Fourth River*. From her dining room table she edits the blog for *Barrelhouse*.

The Treed Lady

Emari DiGiorgio

When the boy in my bible class planted a wad
of Bazooka Joe at the root of my skull, he didn't

expect a sapodilla to grow. Wrist-thick trunk
tangled in tresses overnight, white sap gumming

cotton sheets, my lilac pajama sleeves. Smell
of something sweet, green–not grass or home

of the original mango. A miracle for having
forgiven this boy for putting his hands on me,

no penitence for his trespass in the garden
of my hair. Another tree of knowledge to press

my crown into. Though ruffians teased, would
pin me down, dig nails into the bark banking

my neck, pull sap until it snapped. My new
thirst unimaginable. But there are ways to live

with the gifts we've been given: I cast shade
wherever I picnic, and as the fruits sag heavy

from the upper boughs, I can shake my head,
release their tender yield. As when the sap slips

viscous down my back, my lover scrapes it clean
with a plastic spatula, and we chew for hours.

Emari DiGiorgio is the author of *Girl Torpedo*, the winner of the 2017 Numinous Orison, Luminous Origin Literary Award, and *The Things a Body Might Become*. She's the recipient of the Auburn Witness Poetry Prize, among many others, and a poetry fellowship from the New Jersey State Council on the Arts. She's received residencies from the Vermont Studio Center, Sundress Academy of the Arts, and Rivendell Writers' Colony. She teaches at Stockton University, is a Geraldine R. Dodge Foundation Poet, is the Senior Reviews Editor for *Tupelo Quarterly*, and hosts World Above, a monthly reading series in Atlantic City, NJ.

Amphibian

Lauren K. Carlson

Others prayed as if prayers
were wishes. But I'd
blow out candles before
the song finished.
I learned to plug my nose
and dive, to glide unseen
upstream with salmon,
and make my home among
clusters of egg sac,
stream disturbed with rock
and stem. There, in the ceaseless
whisper of living water, breath
brought me out from under
the lilies. I was cold, struggling
to sing. Sharp light devoured
my gills but the brook bubbled
and the salmon spawned.
Nothing was wishing
except me:
        a frog learning
        to live in two
        worlds at once.

Lauren K. Carlson is a poet and writer, mother and wife, living in Dawson, Minnesota with her husband and three sons. A trained spiritual director, she also produces "Poems from the Field," a web series for Pioneer Public Television exploring poetry and the inner lives of rural Minnesotans. Her work is forthcoming in *Windhover Review, Hermeneutic Chaos,* and previously published in *Mothers Always Write, Heron Tree* and *Blue Heron Review.* She is online at www.laurenkcarlson.com.

Daughter Octopus

Caitlin Thomson

To give birth to another
species, a miracle of the strangest
chord. Certainly a god was involved,
but a god disguised as what? A summer
storm? The back pond? Now I have a child
intended for the ocean in my bathtub.
A husband calling all the zoos
in a rage. A son terrified by his
new sibling and her many
tentacles and suckers.

Caitlin Thomson is the co-founder of The Poetry Marathon, an inter-national writing event. Her work has appeared in numerous anthologies and literary journals including *The Adroit Journal*, *Rust + Moth*, *Barrow Street*, and *Radar*. Learn more at www.caitlinthomson.com.

Butterfly Girl

M. Brett Gaffney

The locker room is as quiet as a centipede.
Training bras hang from hooks like loose teeth.

One girl schlumps in the back corner,
arms wrapped round her body, and cries.
Hair limp as an unwatered houseplant—
it hides her new and sensitive antennae.

The others hear her but keep to themselves,
a flutter of gossip and whispered grass on their knees

They all remember the transformation,
the night their mothers changed the sheets,
red lady lipstick suddenly foreign

                                 and violent.

They quickly dress for gym and fly from the room,
knowing it's best to let alone an empty cocoon,
                dripping wings.

Though none of them admits it, each girl wanted to be alone
when they lost themselves, when their bodies
forced them into a life so unstable
                        and full of wind.

M. Brett Gaffney holds an MFA in Poetry from Southern Illinois University. Her poems have appeared in *Exit 7, Rust+Moth, Permafrost, Devilfish Review, museum of americana, BlazeVOX, Apex Magazine, Tahoma Literary Review,* and *Zone 3,* among others. Her chapbook *Feeding the Dead* (Porkbelly Press) was nominated for a 2018 Elgin Award from the Science Fiction and Fantasy Poetry Association. She works as co-editor of *Gingerbread House* and writes horror genre reviews in her spare time at *No Outlet Horror Reviews.*

The Kestrel Keeps a Girl

Melanie Dunbar

I dive, linger at the door-hook while she finishes breakfast, unlock it with my talons. I envy her long, slim fingers; her spine, sturdy and pliable as any snake I have eaten; her black boots with laces. She roams the meadow flushing grasshoppers, mice and voles for me to eat. I lock the door nights to keep her from coyotes. Through the window, I watch her tend bruising skin. What if I set her free? Don't we mate for life? If she remembers the feel of my wingtips on her cheek, her arms, her thighs, will she return?

Melanie Dunbar tends flowers for a living. She writes her best poetry while weeding someone else's garden. Her poems can be found in *Sweet: A Literary Confection*, *Gargoyle*, and elsewhere. She lives in Southwest Michigan with her family and their rooster, Mr. Beautiful.

The Ex-Girl Begins to Remember That Riff

Minal Hajratwala

They called it *fur* so we would think of cats,
flanks for horses, *horn* for trumpets,
rhinoceri, or high school jazz band
boys in scratchy polyester barely mustaching

reeking testosterone & hope. The first
who held my hand played soprano sax. I jammed
scratch-n-sniff stickers in drawers now crammed
with lingerie & whips, lost track of that

creature filled with grace-notes, formed
of light, not ordinary or even disco shine
but what electrons spark in each other as they pass,
what arcs between the seven million suns,

what jazz I mean real jazz would be if I'd
had ears & not just eyes to see it.

Minal "Write Like a Unicorn" **Hajratwala** is a poet, publisher, author, and writing coach. Her latest book is *Bountiful Instructions for Enlightenment* (2014), published by The (Great) Indian Poetry Collective, a collective press focusing on poetry from global India. Her nonfiction epic *Leaving India: My Family's Journey from Five Villages to Five Continents* won four literary awards, and she is the editor of an anthology, *Out! Stories from the New Queer India.* Join her in unicorn country: www.minalhajratwala.com, or on Twitter @minalh.

Serendipity

Jeannine Hall Gailey

You write your fortune on a five-dollar bill and hand it to the attendant.
The five-dollar bill passes through many hands. They all inherit your fortune.

I believed in magic for long enough that magic became part mindset. I could
speak with animals at the zoo, I could protect people I loved from death. I
conveyed blessings to baby rabbits.

Live long enough and you injure yourself, become unsteady, unstable.
Take time to enjoy the flight, the run through the new grass, that first
strawberry. Because someday, it all will.

Once upon a time a princess. A dragon. Once upon a time you were born, you
were loved and blessed, then stolen by a witch. Once you slew the dragon and
were sad. You wore armor and carried a shining sword. There was a happy
ending, or an unhappy one, depending on the version you discovered.

What can I tell you? My advice has never been practical. Catch the water in
your arms. Hug an armadillo. Tell each snowflake how you love it as it falls.
Your dreams are fish that flash through the water. Be slippery. Be lucky.

Here's your fortune, listen: it's all too fast.

Jeannine Hall Gailey served as Redmond, Washington's second Poet Laureate.
She's the author of five books of poetry: *Becoming the Villainess, She Returns
to the Floating World, Unexplained Fevers, The Robot Scientist's Daughter,*
and *Field Guide to the End of the World*, winner of the Moon City Press Book
Prize. Her work has been featured on NPR's *The Writer's Almanac*, Verse
Daily, and in *The Year's Best Fantasy and Horror*. Her web site is
www.webbish6.com. Her Twitter handle is @webbish6.

Alice Gives Advice to Dorothy

Erin Elizabeth Smith

Never get in a man's hot air balloon—
he'll only take you home

to the family that opened you
to him before. There you are a child

to be tamed, turned into aprons, dustbins,
white pies cooling on windowsills.

He will take your hand and make you
something his, where in this land

you are given a crown, a jeweled walkway,
a horse that flickers deliciously

from one hued gemstone to the next.
And they will lose you again anyhow,

thrown to the slippery sea that opens
its wide maw to devour girls.

What you left to straw men
and clockwork hearts will have been changed

and they will blame the women—the lazy
queens, the mirrored heads of sorceresses

and you, so foolish to believe home
is something you'd want to click your heels for,

a place where we aren't just stories
told to keep girls tight in their own beds.

Erin Elizabeth Smith is the Creative Director at the Sundress Academy for the Arts and the Managing Editor of Sundress Publications and The Wardrobe. She is the author of two full-length collections and the editor of two anthologies; her third collection, *Down: The Alice Poems*, is forth-coming from Agape Editions. Her poems have appeared in numerous journals, including *Ecotone*, *Mid-American*, *Crab Orchard Review*, *Cimarron Review*, and *Willow Springs*, among others. She teaches in the English Department at the University of Tennessee, and in 2017 she was inducted into the East Tennessee Writers Hall of Fame.

Self-Portrait as Judy Garland

Emily Rose Cole

When I was three, my mother caught a bluebird
and stitched her into my throat while I slept, seam

of sinew sewn to wing. Blood pooled into my pillow.
I woke with feathers shot through the sticky ropes of my hair.

At first, I had trouble swallowing, but I learned to gulp
around the beating-hearted bulge beneath my chin.

When she sang, I turned mockingbird, mimicking
her muffled trills, the blue croon of her warbling.

At thirteen, I took off: landed job after job, chased
Benzedrine with Hershey kisses. On nights blurred

salty by vodka and sleeping pills, we'd hum lullabies
in A-minor and I'd finger the scars threaded to my neck,

the ones that held her inside me. At sixteen, I crammed my toes
into a pair of spangled silver heels, threw the deadbolt

across my trailer door. I pried those careful stitches out
with a rust-edged steak knife, and stained my shoes red

as she surged from my mouth, wings oiled in blood,
song bright as polished tin. She was gone

when they found me, escaped out a back window.
She left me with scratches on my cheeks, a throat

full of feathers, and my own precious, blue voice.

Emily Rose Cole is the author of a chapbook, *Love & a Loaded Gun*, from Minerva Rising Press. She has received awards from *Jabberwock Review*, *Philadelphia Stories*, and the Academy of American Poets. Her poetry has appeared or is forthcoming in *Best New Poets 2018*, *Spoon River Poetry Review*, *The Pinch*, and *Southern Indiana Review*, among others. She holds an MFA from Southern Illinois University Carbondale and is pursuing a PhD in Poetry and Disability Studies at the University of Cincinnati. You can reach her via her website at emilyrosecolepoetry.com.

Snow White Explains

Wendy Taylor Carlisle

Try to imagine my danger—
How, when I find them, shape and size don't matter.

How easy then to fall for seven lovers.
How busy every day was with my miners.

How often they would sweet-talk me for favors.

How do they kiss?
They kiss in shifts.
I take their sameness as a gift
and they are generous.
They offer apples first, then more.
There is no rest.
There is no prince.
There never was a prince.

Wendy Taylor Carlisle lives in the Arkansas Ozarks. She is the author of two books, *Reading Berryman to the Dog* and *Discount Fireworks*. and five chapbooks, most recently *They Went Down to the Beach to Play* (2017.) Her work appeared in two anthologies in 2018, *Untold Arkansas* (Et Alia Press) and *50/50* (Quills Edge Press). Her new book, *The Mercy of Traffic*, is due out from Unlikely Books in 2019. For more information, check her website at www.wendytaylorcarlisle.com.

We Are All Her Grandmother

Eileen Malone

We warn her
a young girl does not go
alone into the dark woods

wearing the pre-menstrual
blood-red cloak

unless it is to invite, entice
surrender

we shake our heads
at her pretension of visiting
her grandmother

we are all her grandmother
cut from the wolf's belly
by a passing hunter

eventually red riding hood
will succumb, it's just a matter
of story

and a naturally occurring cycle
of seduction.

Eileen Malone's poetry has been published in over 500 literary journals and anthologies. Her poetry collections include the award winning *Letters with Taloned Claws* (Poets Corner Press), *I Should Have Given Them Water* (Ragged Sky Press), and most recently *It Could Be Me, Although Unsure* (Kelsay Books, Aldrich Press). She's been nominated four times for a Pushcart and lives in the coastal fog at the edge of the San Francisco Bay Area where she directs the Soul-Making Keats Literary Competition she founded over twenty years ago.

Grendel

Mercedes Webb-Pullman

My grandmother's dragon lived
in her kitchen stove, with a black
lighthouse on the oven door.
Grendel breathed flames
and burned if you came too close.

When Grandma baked
she fed pine twigs so the fire
spat and roared, while flour,
sprinkled on an oven tray,
darkened from white
through cream to brown;

hot enough for scones
just before black;
then Grendel starved
and fell silent, smoldering.

Sometimes when I wake
from a dream, as it drains away
I think I can hear

some half-forgotten
starving thing,
still patiently breathing.

Mercedes Webb-Pullman: IIML Victoria University Wellington New Zealand MA in Creative Writing 2011. Her poetry has appeared in *Turbine, 4th Floor, Swamp, Reconfigurations, The Electronic Bridge, Otoliths, Connotations, The Red Room Company, Typewriter, Kind of a Hurricane Press,* and *Cliterature,* among others, and in her books. The latest, *The Jean Genie,* explores the work of Jean Genet through a series of contemporary sonnets. She lives on the Kapiti Coast, New Zealand.

Magical Thinking

Jinn Bug

I can't help my exclaiming
and delight at each little thing,
the stories I invent:
simultaneously peering at what is
and what could be, a devotee
of an imaginary future
snuffing reality so fairytaled
once-upon-a-time and yet-to-come
imaginings are the brightest stars
and each moment of the present
is mythically limned.
There is a curious distance
between me and the moon and
whatever's using me as a tattered
cloak is a merciless shaman,
populating and altering the
alive, vital emptiness
with its own creation.
Few understand conjure-thought
and how would I explain
these ordinary transformations:
Do you see the two clothespins
I left on the line in December?
This one's you and this one's me
holding tight to the icewracked cord
with a hundred thousand ethereal
and necessary hopes filling
the empty space between us.
In the roar of the first January storm
those invisible wishes dance free
and in your dreams you hear
their soft pattering knock
and rise to let them in so the room
glows blue with thaumaturgic light

and the walls dissolve into ruined poems
while a rush of sea salt-spray
dissolves the old pine stairs
and you cannot stop yourself
from calling "Look at this!
Look at this!" while each passerby
ignores two empty clothespins.

Jinn Bug is a poet and visual artist, living on the banks of the mighty Ohio River in Historic Clarksville, IN. Her work has appeared in local, regional and international online and print journals and publications. You can visit her at www.facebook.com/jinnjinn or www.jinnbug.com.

Star Anise

Carol Guess

Today the sky's not making sense. Small dramas unfold in the eaves, woodpeckers fracking the hemlock to fracture. You're standing under controlled bamboo controlling your temper. A little roundabout for the parade, a little whiskey and the night's not over. Trees twine the road to the evening train. Twin coyotes race between two whistles. To cross now would kill me. You're on the other side, summoning red intentions. Even cracked asphalt knows when to stop.

*

My friend texts to say she saw you in a coffee shop on Railroad. You were eating a pastry and drinking a pour over. You were making a ruckus and running a fever. You stole the till, stuffed your shirtsleeves with sugar.

I say you never go to that coffee shop. I say you make coffee with free grounds from the garden shop. I say boiling water, cheesecloth, vamoose!

Vamoose? Why vamoose?

Because my friend didn't see you. Because no one's allowed to see you but me.

*

Tire treads rat us out; no privacy in a city of skylights. You hide in the closet when my ex stops in. Here's a cup of star anise and a saucer of tea. You smell like whiskey, taste like burnt sugar. I only come clean when I wash with you. We sleep on the pier overlooking the river. You with your dander, soft mouth I've made mine.

*

Here's the cemetery where your people were buried, fallen flowers for each unmarked stone. You strike a match for every Mary. In the morning, your truck's left a murder of oil.

*

Woodpeckers drill through the soffits. The attic fills with birds, feathers lofted for liftoff. We stand hand in hand in the birdsong cathedral. Here's where you button my unbuttoned shirt. Flames at the root, at the roof of the tree line: you set love letters on fire in the National Forest. Ash smothers switchbacks. Ceramic squirrels cower in a kingfisher's bower. We spend Saturday lugging fawns off the mountain, plastic hooves oozing onto acorns and twigs.

*

Halfway to nowhere the passenger door unbuckles its lock and threatens to throw me. Side of the road in an unmarked town: 2am, two girls and a pickup. You pull my belt from my jeans in one motion. Tighten the door, lash handle to latch. Tumbleweeds, church spires: no speed limit stops you. Half of this state waits for one careless match. It's true what they say about history repeating. We're locked in a story that circles itself. You promise we'll swerve, head back to the city: delirious green. I wake in Spokane.

*

Stone lions guard the clothesline. My socks dry stiff as two left feet. When we were happy, we danced until the soup caught fire, scraped burn from the bottom of the pot with bread. When Cat wants in, she makes a sound as close to words as need to love. I'm never sure who wanders more; you both stash treasure underground. It's useful knowing CPR. Hearts need reminding when they stop. I grow my hair and scatter crumbs, but nothing gentle leads you home.

Carol Guess is the author of twenty books of poetry and prose, including *Darling Endangered, Doll Studies: Forensics*, and *Tinderbox Lawn*. A frequent collaborator, she writes across genres and illuminates historically marginalized material. In 2014 she was awarded the Philolexian Award for Distinguished Literary Achievement by Columbia University. She teaches at Western Washington University and lives in Seattle.

Visitor at #E504

Karla Linn Merrifield

There she was. Kokopelli, she who appeared,
no warning, from the beyond-beyond, driving
a white '65 Corvette convertible, red leather interior,
the trickster spirit herself in voluptuous flesh
to display at the condo pool day after day, ending
with a skinny dip in the marina with a manatee to kiss,
river toxins no threat to Koko's ravishing pseudo-skin.

Each time for nine days/nights, despite no-pets rules,
she returned dangling a four-foot moccasin she'd trained
to hiss an intricate riddle to earn its keep and hers.
When in April the heavens shine with the sacrificial hair
of the astral queen in her binary-star diadem—
will Aphrodite's coma clusters guide you
downstream on a journey to the cosmic gyre?

She departed, no farewells. No sleek 'Vette
in the guest slot at Bldg. E.'s parking lot.
So like Koko to leave JoJo (and me) attending
to secular speculative myth adorned
in flute music, feathers, a few native
water snakes on the lanai, tamed, but not defanged.
Now her serpents contrive to dance on this page.

Karla Linn Merrifield, a nine-time Pushcart-Prize nominee and National Park Artist-in-Residence, has had 700+ poems appear in dozens of journals and anthologies. She has 13 books to her credit, the newest of which is *Psyche's Scroll*, a book-length poem, published by The Poetry Box Select in June 2018. Forthcoming in Spring 2019 is her full-length book *Athabaskan Fractal: Poems of the Far North*, from Cirque Press. *Her Godwit: Poems of Canada* (FootHills Publishing) received the Eiseman Award for Poetry. She is a frequent contributor to *The Songs of Eretz Poetry Review*, and assistant editor and poetry book reviewer for *The Centrifugal Eye*. She is a member of Just Poets (Rochester, NY), the Florida State Poetry Society, the New Mexico Poetry Society, and The Author's Guild. Visit her at http://karlalinn.blogspot.com. Google her name to learn more; Tweet @LinnMerrifiel.

Ask & Embla

Emily Shearer

Setting: small town community pool
Present: Ask and Embla

Ask and Embla dangled their legs
off the side of Patton Park pool,
wishing for what a watermelon could do
to a dizzying summer day.
Embla made fire from a gaze.
Ask lit the butt of a cigarette he found
near the diving boards.
He cleared his rasp, preparing
to utter the first words ever spoken:

"What's for dinner?"

Then, "So Odin smokes Pall Malls?"
(more of a statement than a question)
And, "Watermelon?"

He liked the unfiltered taste on his lips,
the echo of questions on the back of his throat,
their trill reverberating across the endless blue gloss.

Embla watched a whitening butterfly.
She wanted to know when the ocean
would roil up outside the shell of her body
When gravity would release its stronghold
When the orange trees completed their cycle
would they yield thought or memory.

Ask interrupted her.

"Woman, what to eat?"

She rose, dipped her feet in the water,
baptized herself in the chlorine,
and waited for the transformation.

Emily Shearer is an ex-pat poet who teaches Yoga for Writers and high school French all the while exploring the weight of the word "home." After moving to Prague, Czech Republic with her husband and three children, she now finds herself in the woods outside Houston, Texas. Her poems have been twice nominated for a Pushcart Prize and shortlisted for the Judith B. McCabe Poetry Prize and the University of Houston Robertson Prize. You can find her among the pages of *Ruminate, Clockhouse, emry's journal online, West Texas Literary Review*, and *psaltery&lyre* among others, including her website bohemilywrites.net.

The Newlywed Mermaid

Stacey Balkun

went to Waikiki on her honeymoon
but it felt like a sad imitation

of her hometown. She had expected paradise
to be more humid, more remote.

She bought a hibiscus-printed dress
at an outdoor market that specialized

in selling ocean bones—
whittled coral, puka shells. Plastic

hair clips shaped like plumeria
blossoms. Silk flower leis.

The stench of smoked chicken
and sunscreen hung over

everything. The beach was half
bay and half bathwater, lukewarm

and salted but offering no way
past the breakwater,

a holding pen. Her husband
carried her to water's edge,

a gesture as romantic
as rock wall taming

waves. Sea-become-safety.
Home turned cage.

Stacey Balkun is the author of *Eppur Si Muove*, *Jackalope-Girl Learns to Speak*, and *Lost City Museum*. Winner of the 2017 Women's National Book Association Poetry Prize, her critical and creative work has appeared in *Best New Poets 2018*, *Crab Orchard Review*, *The Rumpus*, and several other anthologies and journals. Chapbook Series Editor for Sundress Publications and a frequent contributor to *The Bind*, Stacey holds an MFA from Fresno State and teaches poetry online at The Poetry Barn and The Loft Literary Center. Visit www.staceybalkun.com.

In the Before

Sara Fetherolf

My mother and I played Thumbelina
at the supermarket. I fit in her purse
just about. I dangled my legs from the cart.
      Only and not oldest daughter, I
      was a thimbleful of saffron then, not
the unbrushed girl she scolded later,

coming into the kitchen to find
I didn't know how to sweep properly.
The broom, unwieldly tall man I danced with,
      hoping if I entranced that skinny djinn,
      and made him eat breadcrumbs from my palm,
the house would never go to wrack.

Atticked, I pined to meet a swallow
who loved me for the crumb I was,
and flew me over the river valley rooftops
      (we were in the East by then),
      over and over
those old highways and those iron

bridges, those bridges, those
bones of giants spanning crownlike
town to town, etchings of my own
      crossings, uncrossings, small the glimmer
      of me again, leaving again
above the expectant water.

Sara Fetherolf's poems and essays have recently appeared in *Tahoma Literary Review*, *Muzzle*, *Iron Horse*, *The California Journal of Poetics*, and *Plath Profiles*, among others. She holds an MFA degree from Hunter College and is currently a Dornsife Fellow in the PhD for Literature and Creative Writing at University of Southern California. She lives in Long Beach, by a half-tamed stretch of ocean.

Monster Charades

Shannon Connor Winward

While we sleep, the things we were afraid of
stay busy in the basements
They go through boxes
They try on old clothes
Their parties are always masquerades
so that when we dream

we don't recognize them
or notice we are still circling
the same rooms draped differently
so we jump when we're supposed to

Sometimes we outgrow them
the bully children, the clowns
and big brown bears
with lethal claws
click-clacking down halls
after the lights go out

and the neighbor girls' mom
who smacked our heads on walls
for squabbling over dolls
and green crayons
Sometimes her mask slips

We are mothers too, now
We understand

and they don't like it
It makes scarecrows of them
scatters their stuffing
and yet they stay
performing the same plays

all the patchwork memories
shredded thin as cobwebs
brittle as vintage Christmas decor
After all

where would they go?
That woman is long dead
of cirrhosis, the kids
have forgotten their names
The stairs don't lead out anymore

(they never did)
and if there were no monsters
to worry and rattle
coffee cans and rusty nails
if nothing ever went bump

or howled down there
we might stop coming
and then what? Imagine
us, all the grownup nightmarers

sleep-walkers exploring
the upstairs places, opening windows
unbarring doors, partying with whatever
comes knocking, 3 AM, the phone ringing
opening our eyes to fear too brazen
to wear a costume
or play games.

Shannon Connor Winward's writing has appeared in *Fantasy & Science Fiction, Analog, The Pedestal Magazine, Lunch Ticket, Minola Review, The Monarch Review, Qu, Literary Mama,* and elsewhere. She is author of the Elgin-award winning chapbook *Undoing Winter* and winner of a 2018 Delaware Division of the Arts Emerging Artist Fellowship. In between parenting, writing and other madness, Shannon is also Founding Editor of *Riddled with Arrows,* a literary journal dedicated to metafiction, ars poetica, and writing that celebrates the process and product of writing as art. Her first full-length poetry collection, *The Year of the Witch,* was recently released from Sycorax Press.

Letter to the Gnome Who Stole My Firstborn

Shelley Puhak

Can I bring you a better bird,
perhaps a talking hawk?
A golden stew-pot? Might we still
negotiate?

My dear *rumpled-sheets,*
house-on-stilts, donkey-skin:
I would have written sooner,
had I the flour and fat

to make the words. Yesterday
it rained the primordial
roux, the A C G U proteins,
base of the mother sauce,

two consonants, two vowels—
tin and gut, metal
and mineral in the volcanic
vent of mouth. Yesterday

we met at that dressing room
entrance. I was seeking
a shirt for his funeral and you
were smirking at my deflated

belly: *you're pregnant!*
You caught me with a handful
of maternity shirts
struggling to find something

that would fit: *no, not*
pregnant. What is the name
for what I am now—full
of the vast gaps

between the smallest
spaces, the pinky's width
between two slabs
of granite meeting up

at the sea? Remember
how we met
at that animal sanctuary, among
caged rabbits, kenneled dogs?

You were minding falcons,
dwarfed by their tall
netted towers. My offering—
a fledgling, found half-hairless

and fly-swarmed.
Yet it lived.
My dear rock-spawn, root-
resident, underground-ether—

did you want more
than an ordinary starling?

Shelley Puhak is the author of two poetry collections, the more recent of which, *Guinevere in Baltimore*, was selected by Charles Simic for the Anthony Hecht Poetry Prize. Her poems have appeared in *Kenyon Review Online, Missouri Review, North American Review,* and *Verse Daily*.

How To Housebreak a Shadow

Carolyn Moore

After catastrophe, subside in silk
beneath harsh lights and over the day's fresh
newspapers spread across the floor.

During this convalescent sprawl, console
the shadow sniffing, cowering, at your feet.
Pat it and point the papers out.

Tell it the intricate, shadow-free frost etched
on your pane is winter's fleeting jealousy.
Coax and hoist its confidence.

Push its nose in each failure—yet grant
it stints of bliss and frolic, at the end
of the mindful leash that scolds *restraint*.

Once it shows (fractured and ambivalent)
collared obedience, reward it. Call it
Grief and feed it beneath your sink.

Carolyn Moore's four chapbooks won their competitions. Her book, *What Euclid's Third Axiom Neglects To Mention about Circles*, won the White Pine Press Poetry Prize. She taught at Humboldt State University (Arcata, California). Now a freelance writer and researcher, she works from the last vestige of the family farm in Tigard, Oregon.

Sciomancy

Miriam Bird Greenberg

My usual name had left me—gone up a panther trail, a hog path
        through the gap where my great aunt had lived when she lost a bunch
of boys

to TB—and I was out with my bicycle to find red nettle and fevergrass,
        to get better and bring it back

before my death name took hold. I'd joined the church
        fifty-seven times I guess when I was a little girl, but
    none of it ever took.

    Sometimes when I lay in bed and ate nothing
but a spoonful of sugar with a little camphor I would wake to hear my ghost

walking around in the dark. Get up right now, I'd tell myself, and I'd brew
coffee
        on the woodstove and stay up calling him
back. One time

    we got to fussing and by dawn he'd left. He got to where you couldn't
tell him
nothing, but soon enough my right name

would return from the hollows whistling a tune and I would feel my skin set
true,
        and know it was the death-name that had
died and was the dead one.

    When I rode through the chills lost
in the bottomlands and said not a word so none would recognize my voice,

just past there lay the leafless tree and the unlettered stones. The pasture wild with blackberries,

and knotted around the knees of milk cows, blacksnakes drinking from their
udders.

> There, my death-name, sitting on a stump to
> pass the time.

Miriam Bird Greenberg is the author of *In the Volcano's Mouth,* winner of
the 2015 Agnes Lynch Starrett Prize, and the chapbooks *All night in the new
country* and *Pact-Blood, Fevergrass.* A poet with a fieldwork-derived practice,
she's written about the nomads, hitchhikers, and hobos living on America's
margins. A high school dropout and former hitchhiker herself, she's held
fellowships from the NEA, the Poetry Foundation, and the Provincetown Fine
Arts Work Center. She's currently at work on a manuscript about the economic
migrants and asylum seekers of Hong Kong's Chungking Mansions. A former
Wallace Stegner Fellow, in 2017 she was a writer-in-residence at the National
University of Singapore and last year at the Jan Michalski Foundation in
Switzerland. She lives in the San Francisco Bay Area, where for many years
she collaboratively developed site-specific performances for very small
audiences. In 2020 she's scheming to ride her bicycle along the route of the
historic Silk Road.

She Stands

Cecilia Woloch

My friend, who is silver this spring. Who is gamine and slender and silver as birch. Whose hair is cropped short as a boy's, bristling and sharp. Who stands tall as a tree. My friend who is silver this spring in each cell of her body, and gamine as birch. Her eyes like two birds, like twin *tra-la-la-la's*; silver brimming the edges of them. My friend who stands slender, lashed in wind, her lover cinching her belt at her waist. His hands at her waist as the wind would be. Who has pressed his mouth to the mouth of prayer each night in secret while she's slept: *that she not wake in fever; not wake in pain.* My friend who all this winter past wore needles in her blood. Felt the weight of her long hair dying when she tried to lift her head. Felt, in her long limbs, darkness pool. And now she's risen, slender, silver, leaf and shadow, bends like birch. Leans down to kiss me. Turns in the wind and kisses her lover where he stands. Who all our lives believed in beauty's beating back of death. Until now, as the rain begins, as she lets the sky pour into her.

Cecilia Woloch has published six collections of poems — most recently *Earth*, (Two Sylvias Press) —and a novel, *Sur la Route* (Quale Press). Recent honors include a fellowship from the National Endowment for the Arts, a Fulbright fellowship and a Pushcart Prize. She collaborates regularly with artists in other disciplines and conducts workshops for writers around the world.

Combing the Bones of Our Vows

Colette Inez

Veronica, lavender,
        geranium, rose,
there's a cricket
        in the wicker chair, a muddle
of summer rooms

where nobody warns me
        in days to come the cresting
letters will slump to one,
        none, in a winter of dull
turnings.

The baa of words.
        There's a stammering lamb
in the cage of my throat.
        Close your mystery
when I talk. These yawning
        chronicles go on,

and gone to catch a time to burn
        the sun rolls under the world.
Has anyone told the crocus
        the snow's last fall won't harm
the crops? Who will tell
        the pisspoor mouse?

Alchemist, alchemist, we spin
        what we are into a crucible—
gold leaves and bitter light
        combing the bones of our vows.

Colette Inez published eleven collections and won Guggenheim and Rockefeller awards, plus two NEA fellowships and Pushcart prizes. *The Secret of M. Dulong*, a memoir released by The University of Wisconsin Press, was followed in 2015 by *The Luba Poems* from Red Hen Press. She long taught at Columbia University and is widely anthologized.

Witching

Robin A. Sams

She stirs the pot   wooden spoon three times
clockwise   nine times counterclockwise
staring at the yellowed wall
between stove and fan vent
drips of dried oil splashes of dinners past
unclean
her eyes drift
three times clockwise   nine times counter
she remembers other Sundays
                    ancient Sundays
sitting in stiff-backed pews
blue-bound book in her hands   bigger than her hands
she twisted her eyes through the pages
the words a brimstone
filling her with warmth from the bottom up
she dropped it once while the man
white-robed and mid-fire
froze
at the sound   an echoing thud like a final heartbeat
like a death knell
her mother going red beside her
as she fumbled to the floor to pick it up
and stayed there
and the singing   the singing she liked best
a disharmony of voices daring the heavens to listen
three times clockwise   nine times counter
the summer she found God in a blonde girl's kiss
the Fourth of July firework night she found
                    more of wonder under that same girl's butterfly dress

and she never went back to the pews
but a blue-bound book slipped under her bed   forgotten
eventually   covered in dust   becoming the dust
she untwists the bun of her hair
black coils uncoiling   dipping
into the pot
three times clockwise   nine times counter
eye of frog   or   slime of bog
tincture of labia   penny-pinch of freedom
a sip for taste   a sip for luck.

Robin A. Sams lives in Nanaimo, B.C., Canada, where she hoards books and men. Her work has appeared in a variety of publications, including *Island Writer* magazine and *Unrequited: An Anthology of Love Poems About Inanimate Objects*. Find her blog here: http://robinasams.wordpress.com.

The Town Witch Tries to Make Friends

Jill Crammond

She offers her left arm,
her good arm,
her casting spells arm.
She opens

wide her perfect mouth
veils the sharp tips of her teeth
with a clean tongue,
speaks in the gibberish of women.

She promises not to eat their husbands
or handle their food,
dirty their laundry or covet their gardens.

As usual she has it all wrong.

As usual the men do not cooperate.
Three of them have offered to kiss her
behind their tool sheds,

in the back seats of their cars,
under cover of a new moon.
When you are not a wife,
but a witch

even your own shadow blushes
in your company,
prefers you enter through the back door,
rolls up the *Welcome* mat

should you mention stopping by.
Your name is always spelled wrong
or when it is carved into the base of a tree,
the kitchen knife it was carved with

always the dullest blade slipped
back into the drawer
when the real wife
is making dinner.

Jill Crammond is a poet/mother/artist, feeding her children and funding her passion for poetry by teaching art & writing. Her work has appeared in various journals and anthologies, including *Fire on Her Tongue* (Two Sylvia's Press), *B* (Kind of a Hurricane Press), *Hi Honey, I'm Home* (Wordland 2), and *Thirty Days: The Best of the Tupelo Press 30/30 Project's First Year*.

Menopause at the Market

Patricia J. Esposito

At the bin of tomatoes, the ripe
avocados, his hands work, slick
palm over polished skins,
the black-green of forest earth
and the red pulp of sunlight.

I think each fruited orb
appears at his tender touch,
created by this careful god,
whose brown fingers caress
and ripen for seeding what he sees.

With his head bent to the task,
his night hair is an illusion,
a shade for hazel-sun eyes,
as he creates and colors
a world flavor-spiked.

And I stand stunned
to disintegrate, harvested
too long ago, remembering
sunlight and soil and the male
touch that makes a seed bloom.

Patricia J. Esposito's work appears in a range of anthologies and journals, including *Blurring the Line, Clarify, Stories of Music, Scarlet Literary Magazine,* and *Clean Sheets.* She finds inspiration in the passion of music, in striking images and words, and in those extraordinary occasions when grace and beauty pass through.

Baucis and Philemon

Kate Hovey

> *The peasants in that district show the stranger*
> *The two trees close together, and the union*
> *Of oak and linden in one. The ones who told me*
> *The story, sober ancients, were no liars,*
> *Why should they be? And my own eyes have seen...*

Ovid, *The Metamorphoses*, Book VIII

Translated by Rolphe Humphries

Regulars, the senior crowd, nod as they pass,
Witnesses to their weekly pilgrimage: back-corner
Booth beneath an arbor of plastic grapes,

Dust catcher she calls it, measuring her steps
Beside him, he, tethered to oxygen tank and walker—
Go on, old gal—never uses her given name.

Obliging, she totters ahead, eases dry bones
Over the banquette's cracked vinyl as—unbidden—
A platter appears, their usual antipasto,

Ice water, bottomless basket of warm bread,
A brimming half-carafe of house Chianti.
She pours; he settles in. They raise their glasses,

Share prosciutto, pitted olives, provolone,
Eavesdrop on the family one booth over,

toast again. No talk—no need, for those two.

The waitress breezes by, *Everything good?*
Is now, he winks, gives her that satyr's smile.
Oh, Phil! his wife mock-scolds, their joke for ages,

Though once upon a time it wasn't funny.
She'd rage over trysts she knew of, ones she guessed,
Sleuthing for strands of hair, a scent—tough years—

Packed up the car and kids, once, headed home,
But her mother, fierce as Cerberus, barred the doorway.
Sent back to that living hell *for the sake of the babies,*

She nearly drowned in a river of wine, red Lethe.
Her firm belief in the fairy tale pulled her through it;
That, and the photo long hidden under lingerie.

Now, the mortgage paid, the children distant,
She still marks time in diapers, laundered sheets—
Nothing new. All men are infants, really.

Who'll care for her the way she's cared for him?
Her one bright hope, that they'll go out together,
Rises like a prayer through the cobwebbed lattice.

Ready? he asks, cash laid on the table.
Seated, he looks much younger, shoulders broad,
Back straight as the columns painted just behind him,

The mural, a rustic scene with a ruined temple,
So real, she thinks she hears its pine boughs whisper.
Ready she sighs. Her gnarled hands reach for his.

The tips of their crooked fingers lace together—
Last touch before the cool bark closes over,

And green leaves—real ones—fill that dusty arbor.

Kate Hovey is the author of three award-winning books of poetry for young readers: *Arachne Speaks* (2001), *Ancient Voices* (2004) and *Voices of the Trojan War* (2004), published by Simon and Schuster. A mask maker and metalsmith, she performs and conducts workshops at schools across the country, using poetry, myth and the art of the mask to bring the gods and heroes of ancient Greece to life for students of all ages. A contributor to *Women Versed in Myth: Essays on Modern Poets* (McFarland), her "grown-up" poems have appeared most recently in *PoemMemoirStory, So To Speak, subTerrain, Switched-on Gutenberg, The River Styx* and in the anthologies *In The Words of Womyn* (Yellow Chair Press) and *The Lyric Moment* (Tebot Bach). Visit www.KateHovey.com for more information on her books and programs.

Gesso

Sandra Anfang

At the hospice thrift store
a green and gold frame with rococo carvings
called to me—*Hey lady, over here.*
I swear I heard The Fisherman,
name emblazoned on the back in white chalk,
tap out a message in some harbor code.

Just an average Joe packing wooden crates
some stacked high behind his right shoulder
nothing much to look at—
Fortuna at lip, its hanging ash the most arresting point,
no fish graced the table where he worked.

I took him home
greedy for the large canvas
nicely framed & linen lipped
ignoring the keen resemblance to an old friend
four years dead who kept a funky wooden boat
and fished for fun.

I had worked on that boat
helped to sand and prime her hull
stroked her lineage
helped make her seaworthy.
Forgetting all this
I went right on laying gesso
hefting my brush with abandon
hungry for a blank surface
on which to plant my vision.

The signature flashed like a neon sign
a noted Spaniard thirty years gone
had dashed it off in a burst of passion
just as I was wont to do.

How hungry we are to pave over
erase the past
begin anew.

Tall pillars now cover the fisherman;
a stone wall blocks his crates.
When you close your eyes
you can smell the smoke from his cigarette.

Sandra Anfang is a Northern California poet and visual artist. Her poems have appeared in numerous journals, including *San Francisco Peace and Hope*, *Unbroken Literary Journal*, *Rattle*, and *Spillway*. She is the author of *Looking Glass Heart* and *Road Worrier: Poems of the Inner and Outer Landscape* (Finishing Line Press) and *Xylem Highway* (Main Street Rag). Sandra has been nominated for a Best Short Fictions award and a Pushcart Prize. She is founder and host of the monthly poetry series, Rivertown Poets, in Petaluma, California, and a California Poet/Teacher in the Schools.

A Modern-day Amazon Visits the Museum of Fine Arts, Houston

Beatriz F. Fernandez

"Sarcophagus Depicting a Battle Between Soldiers and Amazons, 140–170 A.D."

Where have you gone, all my sisters?
From these marble veins your blood
won't spill as it once did –
on that faraway plain
we tested our battle axes and spears
against Roman swords and plated armor—

Not fated to be our finest hour,
great Athena turned her face aside
and heeded not our battle cries.
Overcome and taken captive—
we would sooner fall on our swords
than be bound by men.

Sleep, sisters. Let not the pounding hooves
nor the clash of steel against shield open your eyes,
nor let the cries of the wounded
stir you from slumber—though I heed them all—
I must, for I'm the last of our kind.

When you awaken, Hippolyte's daughters,
you will walk with the lady of the white halls,
where once you rode bare-breasted
across sweet-smelling hayfields,
the sun always at your back,

your shields ever at the ready.

Alone now, I fear my heart has fled this field
where I must once more face an enemy—
fiercer yet than Caesar's men—
who yields a javelin more formidable
than any we could have met in battle—
with a thrust deeper than death.

Beatriz F. Fernandez is the author of *The Ocean Between Us* (Backbone Press) and *Shining from a Different Firmament* (Finishing Line Press), which she presented at the Miami Book Fair International. She has read her poetry on WLRN, South Florida's NPR news station and was the grand prize winner of the 2nd annual Writer's Digest Poetry Award. Her poems have appeared in *Falling Star Magazine* (2014 Pushcart Nomination), *Label Me Latina/o*, *Minerva Rising*, *Thirty West Publishing House* (2017 Pushcart Nomination), *Verse Wisconsin*, and *Writer's Digest*, among others. Contact her via @nebula61 or visit www.beasbooks.blogspot.com.

Lady Macbeth On Call-in Radio

Dori Appel

When I've got my hands and arms
soaped up, they look exactly
like the long white gloves I wore
to dances long ago. Still,
things never come out right. I mean,
after all the lathering and rinsing,
drying should be a celebration,
not some threadbare afterthought!
Sometimes I dream of great soft towels,
the colors of jewels or blood, then wake
with terror pulsing at my throat
until I find a cigarette and turn on
the radio. In the dreams I love the best,
I'm watching through a washer's
sudsy window while a hundred gloves
swoop round and round like a flight
of butterflies. I find it very soothing,
but tonight the gloves began to crash
into the window and the room filled up
with so much steam that I could barely see
a metal table stacked almost
to the ceiling with a mountain of
stained gloves. Suddenly, the pile
fell on me, dirty gloves clinging like
hungry, sucking mouths,
and I knew with hopeless certainty
that I'd never be allowed to leave
until I figured out the way
to make them clean again.

Dori Appel's poems have been widely published in magazines and anthologies, as well as in her collection of poems, *Another Rude Awakening* (Cherry Grove Collections). A playwright as well as a poet, she is the author of many published plays and monologues, and was the winner of the Oregon Book Award in Drama in 1998, 1999, and 2001. She lives and writes in Ashland, Oregon. Visit http://www.doriappel.com.

Toll

Laura Madeline Wiseman

The interstate slows. It's a work zone. The weather is bad, visibility limited—snow, sleet, black ice, taillights before us, people in the ditch. When we got on, we had to pay. When we stopped for gas, we paid. Every twenty miles, we pay again. *Give me the wallet,* you say. *Do you have any cash?* I don't carry cash. I don't carry a wallet with an ID. If I got hit by a troll, I'd be just another dead woman on the road. Last night, you told me you did not eat the troll mushrooms you found in the backyard this summer. Last week, you said you didn't stop at that border shop with troll truffles, troll hash, and troll brownies with cashew frosting. This morning, you said a new brewery was brewing troll beer. *Is that right?* I said, hoping it wasn't. I give you our change from the console, the ones from the wallet, a credit card when all that's gone. You grip the wheel, veins popping, something stone about your jaw. I want to ask how to pay the toll just ahead. We slow. You say, *Give me your wedding ring.* I do.

Laura Madeline Wiseman's poetry has appeared in *Strange Horizons, Abyss & Apex, Gingerbread House Literary Magazine, Red Rose Review, Star*Line, Silver Blade*, and elsewhere. Her latest book is *What a Bicycle Can Carry* (BlazeVOX [books]).

Change of Plan

Jane Frank

I'll go to work.
This June day is a trick,
the frangipani
takes Escher steps
across a sky in hiding,
wind juggling leaves
above a frosted brick maze,
palm trees photoshopped in,
the sun blindfolded.
I can see a hat moving
along the fence palings:
the ghost of the man next door
is mowing his invisible lawn.
A medley of soccer balls,
tennis balls, frisbees
bullets and arrows
return through the gloom
like space junk.
The postman almost collides
with the mad woman
from up the street
who, jumping dog mess
in her black flapping coat,
mutters a spell
to rid the world of evil,
bags of dry-cleaning
trailing her like a snake.
It all started
when my husband said

rats were gnawing
in his dreams
and could I call
the pest control people?
That was when I thought
I heard the possums talking,
quietly, then pausing
as though, at any moment,
a normal Brisbane day
might reappear.

Jane Frank lives and writes in Brisbane, Australia, where she teaches in creative industries and literary studies at Griffith University. Her work has recently appeared in *Antipodes, Takahe, Not Very Quiet, Algebra of Owls, Stilts Journal, Hecate* as well as in a number of other anthologies including *Heroines* (Neo Perennial Press), *Travellin' Mama* (Demeter Press) and *Pale Fire: New Writings on the Moon* (Frogmore Press). Her chapbook *Milky Way of Words* is available from Ginninderra Press. http://janefrankpoetry.wordpress.com.

The Goner

Carolyn Hembree

They'll read something like it somewhere—
wronged one longed all along for the long gone wrong one

wool over this one's eyes, steel wool
in that one's mouth, a half-eaten blood orange

on the floor of some abode, some dust
devil of angel dust, where, half-senseless

in a half-slip, a drama mama fans herself
with an automatic, strung along

by this mind reader, that peter
meter, another string bikini'd string bean

who in a string of bad language unstrung
my mind—a gripe a gulp a growl a glint a goring.

Carolyn Hembree was born in Bristol, Tennessee. Her debut poetry collection, *Skinny*, came out from Kore Press. Trio House Books published her second collection, *Rigging a Chevy into a Time Machine and Other Ways to Escape a Plague*, winner of the Trio Award and the Rochelle Ratner Memorial Award. Her work has appeared in *Colorado Review*, *Drunken Boat*, *The Journal*, *Poetry Daily*, and other publications. She has received grants and fellowships from PEN, the Louisiana Division of the Arts, and the Southern Arts Federation. An associate professor at the University of New Orleans, Carolyn teaches writing and serves as poetry editor of *Bayou Magazine*.

Amberwing

Sandra Marchetti

Perithemis tenera

Hover over me,
fat-beaded miracle.

Swell your breast
clustered between

red-tinged wings
in autumn nearly

done opening.
Scan the grass

one last time,
dry as a stone,

as a woman alone,
climbing the stairs,

landing nowhere.

Sandra Marchetti is the author of *Confluence*, a full-length collection of poetry (Sundress Publications). She is also the author of four chapbooks of poetry and lyric essays, including *Heart Radicals* (About Editions), *Sight Lines* (Speaking of Marvels Press), *A Detail in the Landscape* (Eating Dog Press), and *The Canopy (*MWC Press). Sandra's poetry appears widely in *Poet Lore*, *Blackbird*, *Ecotone*, *Southwest Review*, *River Styx*, and elsewhere. Her essays can be found at *The Rumpus*, *Whiskey Island*, *Mid-American Review*, *Barrelhouse*, *Pleiades*, and other venues. Sandy earned an MFA in Creative Writing—Poetry from George Mason University and now serves as the Coordinator of Tutoring Services at the College of DuPage in the Chicagoland area.

Adam Thinking

Catherine Moore

---

after Lucille Clifton

She is daughter of a woman almost named Madonna
one sister in a tribe of brothers, stolen from bone
word-eater, kitchen alchemist, is it any wonder
the wind and sea hungers to tunnel back
inside desperate for manly and bitter wish,
dark and loyal to reconnect rib and clay
to spirit the house, to be whole again.

She is some need, some quiet on the street
struggling to roar through a mouth
into a name, a fog over land,
fire into air, this fierce creation
is genesis rather than born.

Lyricist and fiction writer **Catherine Moore** is a recipient of the *Southeast Review*'s Gearhart Prize for Poetry. She is the author of *ULLA! ULLA!* and three chapbook collections. Her work appears in *Tahoma Literary Review, Southampton Review, Mid-American Review, Broad River Review* and in various anthologies, including the juried *Best Small Fictions*. She has been awarded Walker Percy and Hambidge fellowships; her honors also include a Nashville MetroArts grant as well as Pushcart, the Best of the Net, and VERA Award nominations. Unsolicited Press will publish her upcoming collection of lyrical pieces in the voices of bog bodies.

Mermaid

Theresa Davis

---

then there are days when the waves overtake me
usually in the mornings when the stucco ceiling writhes
an ocean over my head the covers become so heavy
I cannot free myself from the undertow of memories
all this sand in my hair in my bed

I rise anyway because that is what you do when you have
mouths to feed and you have these legs you wanted
so desperately, you traded them for silence.

Theresa Davis teaches poetry to youth and adults in the Atlanta Area. In 2002, Theresa joined forces with her mother and brother to form the spoken word performance group MoDaSo (Mother/ Daughter/ Son) and released two music CD's *This is for Family* and *The Uncivil War*. She has self-published several collections of poetry including *Rock Star Poet, Head Games* and *Simon Says*. Theresa won the Women of the World Poetry Slam Champion title, among numerous awards and honors. In 2013, Sibling Rivalry Press published *After This We Go Dark*. Her poems were also published in *Flicker and Spark, This Assignment is so Gay*, and *G.R.I.T.S. Girls Raised In The South*.

Owl

Jane Morgan

---

after Allen Ginsberg

I saw the best clothes of the next generation destroyed by fences, shredded
       torn open, dragged past wire in paddocks looking for a friendly
       frog,
Angel-haired children playing in mud the connection to Dynamo and Napisan
       in my washing-machinery tonight,
who poverty and tatters and hollow-eyed and tired sat up sewing in the
       supernatural quietness of late-hour sleeping family brick veneer
       struggling with blind needle knotted cotton contemplating sleep,
who bared her teeth to heaven under the southern cross and found no
       matching socks and none clean to be partnered,
who thirsts for selfish time an hour with no distractions
       hallucinating morning now it's night with tragedy of ironing
       looming,
who presses school culottes inside-out with fierce creases and no seam-shine,
whose mind though still alive eschews originality, Allen Ginsberg forgive me
       isolated regional mother braced beneath great night of southbound
       stars,
who profanes your sacred words with my mundane; from your dais amongst
       the holies read what thoughts I have of you tonight as worship,
who falls into bed at dawn in underwear, burning hours in resentful
       domesticity and listening to chatting Furbys through the wall,
who mourns the prayer quenched mute beneath avalanche of unfolded towels
       uniforms hand-washed jumpers willfully unknitting in crevasses,
who casts weary mind-lines testing the waters of tomorrow,
who accepts that it may be today's kind sibling maybe its evil twin,
amoral psychopathic day kicking holes in walls vomiting in corners
       tiny hours scurrying across the floor desperate buzzing morning
       caught in web,
who, shamed on presentation day, baked only two plates of cupcakes, arriving
       late with leprous icing still oozing,

who was stared down by other mothers in pride of swirls, fondant flowers and
      cachous,
presentation day is purgatory, a waking nightmare smiling nodding chat
      pretending not to not know names, inspiration strikes from
      nowhere and instantly recoils, who is her partner is that their son,
intolerable blind hour of whispering child-choir and speeches and mind
      leaping towards a kind of comprehension claimed by the Time
      which sucks like quicksand between destiny and duties,
coffee mental clarity, backyard green tree snake in the trellis walls, whine
      emptiness over everything, sunblind shopfronts already the 3
      o'clock joyride lollypop lady stop sign zebra crossing, mindless
      veering into road in the roaring afternoon sun of sub-tropical
      country town,
cul-de-sac cricket rantings and child kings of the street, who do not tire of
      endlessly running shouting from boundary to holy stumps on Milo
      until the noise of ice-cream truck brings them out roistering mouth-
      dry and hungry and all but drained of pocket money in the clear
      light of afternoon,
who disperse at dinner time and talk all night of desolate homework questions
      detonating parents' crack of doom,
my children talk continuously for seven hours from school to bed and in their
      sleep dreaming of the local museum and Federation Bridge,
a small battalion of platonic conversationalists calling out long after bedtime,
      fast asleep,
yacketayakking screaming sometimes whispering facts and memories and
      unseen visitors and I drag in each time to check if dream has given
      way to fear,
then back to work, tired husband mired in sleep at last whose wife no
      company finally attains the gaunt triumph of defeating this week's
      laundry.

*Source texts: Ginsberg, A, 'Howl' and 'A
Supermarket in California', Howl and Other Poems,
City Lights Books, 2006.*

Jane Morgan completed her BA in Writing at Southern Cross University in
2016. She lives with her musician husband and their two daughters in a
nominally utopian township on the NSW far north coast, where truth is elusive
and far stranger than fiction.

Acknowledgements

in order of anthology appearance

Weitzman, Sarah Brown. "Forbidden." *AWP Chronicle,* September 1983.

Givhan, Jennifer. "A Woman Might Want to Fly, Away." *Crab Creek Review*.

Gerkensmeyer, Sarah. "The Woman Whistles." *B O D Y.*

Kyle, Catherine. "Ode to a Parallel Universe in Which I Make My Point." *Midwestern Gothic,* reprinted in *Parallel* by Another New Calligraphy, 2017.

Benedetti, Tammy. "2.3". *Poison in Small Doses*, Lithic Press, 2018.

Chang, Kristin. "Madame Butterfly." *Rookie,* 2015.

Anderson, E. Kristin. "Tupperware Party." *Otis Nebula*; reprinted by Hermeneutic Chaos Press.

Chronister, Jan. "Singer." *Caught between Coasts*, Clover Valley Press.

Fordon, Kelly. "Gina 1: 22 Ballard Avenue." *Amarillo Bay Literary Journal,* Volume 12; reprinted by Standing Rock Cultural Arts in *On the Street Where We Live,* 2011.

Vignali, Elizabeth. "The Fates Hang Wallpaper." *Clover*, A Literary Rag.

Bella, Lanna. "My Anguished Goulash." *Alexandria Quarterly*.

King, Hilary. "Why I Have Five Calendars in My Kitchen." *The Maid's Car*, Aldrich Press/Kelsay Books.

Dhar, Nandini. "History's Private Life." *Quiddity*.

Sherbow, Jackie. "Trade." *Emotive Fruition* performance series, NYC.

Palacio, Melinda. "The Mermaid of California." *Mockingheart Review*; reprinted in *Bird Forgiveness, 3: A Taos Press*.

Mali, Marie-Elizabeth. "If the ocean had a mouth." Academy of American Poets *Poem-A-Day* series on March 26, 2014.

Hurter, Jade. "The Minotaur." *Columbia Poetry Review*.

Neves, PaulA. "Capricornucopia (The Dream of the Goats)." *Writers of the Portuguese Diaspora in the United States and Canada: An Anthology*.

Rich, Susan. "Tricks a Girl Can Do." *Cloud Pharmacy*, White Pine Press, 2014.

Atkinson Mercer, Melissa. "My tongue hatched; all at once." *Rust & Moth*.

Erickson, Susan. "Venus de Milo Gets Ready for the Halloween Party." *Lauren Bacall Shares a Limousine*, Brick Road Press.

DiGiorgio, Emari. "The Treed Lady." *Connotation Press: An Online Artifact*.

Carlson, Lauren. "Amphibian." *Animals I Have Killed,* The Comstock Review Press, 2019.

Gaffney, M. Brett. "Butterfly Girl." *Glint*.

Gailey, Jeannine Hall. "Serendipity." *Interfictions*.

Smith, Erin Elizabeth. "Alice Gives Advice to Dorothy." *Palooka*.

Cole, Emily Rose. "Self-Portrait as Judy Garland." *Jabberwock Review.*

Webb-Pullman, Mercedes. "Grendel." *Walt's Corner.*

Guess, Carol. "Star Anise." *The Reckless Remainder*, Noctuary Press, 2017.

Shearer, Emily. "Ask & Embla." *Silver Birch.*

Puhak, Shelley. "Letter to the Gnome Who Stole My Firstborn." *Poemeleon 11,* reprinted by Broadview Press in *Writing and Workshopping Poetry: A Constructive Introduction.* Ed. Stephen Guppy, 2016.

Moore, Carolyn. "How to Housebreak a Shadow." *The Bellevue Literary Review.*

Greenberg, Miriam Bird. "Sciomancy." *Shankpainter 5,* reprinted by Ricochet Press in *Pact-Blood, Fevergrass,* 2013.

Woloch, Cecilia. "She Stands." *TAB: A Journal of Poetry & Poetics.*

Inez, Colette. "Combing the Bones of Our Vows." *The Southern Review.*

Hovey, Kate. "Baucis & Philemon." *River Styx.*

Appel, Dori. "Lady MacBeth on Call-in Radio." *Seems and Inside Out: Literature of Mental Illness*, Miami University Press.

Frank, Jane. "Change of Plan." *Morphrog.*

Hembree, Carolyn. "The Goner." *Skinny,* Kore Press.

Marchetti, Sandra. "Amberwing." *Still: The Journal* and *Heart Radicals,* ELJ Publications, 2016.

Moore, Catherine. "Adam Thinking." *Caesura: The Journal of Poetry Center San José.*

Davis, Theresa. "Mermaid." *Drowned: A Mermaid's Manifesto*, Sibling Rivalry Press, 2016.

CPSIA information can be obtained
at www.ICGtesting.com
Printed in the USA
FFHW010903221019
55659112-61487FF